VAGINA HOMOGENEITY

OLOLADE AYANNIYI

authorHOUSE®

AuthorHouse™ UK
1663 Liberty Drive
Bloomington, IN 47403 USA
www.authorhouse.co.uk
Phone: 0800.197.4150

Published by AuthorHouse 09/04/2015

ISBN: 978-1-5049-8937-4 (sc)
ISBN: 978-1-5049-8938-1 (hc)
ISBN: 978-1-5049-8939-8 (e)

Print information available on the last page.

Any people depicted in stock imagery provided by Thinkstock are models,
and such images are being used for illustrative purposes only.
Certain stock imagery © Thinkstock.

This book is printed on acid-free paper.

Because of the dynamic nature of the Internet, any web addresses or
links contained in this book may have changed since publication and may
no longer be valid. The views expressed in this work are solely those
of the author and do not necessarily reflect the views of the publisher,
and the publisher hereby disclaims any responsibility for them.

Scripture quotations marked NKJV are taken from the New
King James Version. Copyright © 1982 by Thomas Nelson,
Inc. Used by permission. All rights reserved.

ACKNOWLEDGMENT

I say a big thank you to the Author of life for making this masterpiece a reality.

Patrick Mcbane, of Transformational Leadership inc. USA, and CEO Market Place Solution Inc., USA.

CONTENTS

PROLOGUE

You had me so don't have me again
Duplicating me amount to waste of Resources.
I am that and that is me, I am one and the same
I am homogeneous I am the same, I am exact, I am identical.
The purpose I serve is the purpose my identical twin serves.
The way I react is the way my identical twin reacts.

We both smile the same way
We both cry the same way
We both sing the same way
We both dance the same way
We both sleep the same way
We both walk the same way.

Acquiring her is acquiring me
Contentment is a great gain
Resources once squander may never be sourced back.
Don't squander your resources over identical products
Our resources are from the same source, THE SOURCE.
The Source only produces the same resources
Resources sourced from this source are the same.

Purpose is the reason behind every action
Proposing without purpose is pointless.
Any action without a purpose is purposeless.
The purpose for having me is to serve a purpose
The purpose that I serve is the purpose that they serve
We are homogeneous.

Vagina Homogeneity

Multiplying me in multiples multiple your sorrow.
I said we are the same
She said we are the same
He said we are the same
They said we are the same
We said we are the same,

Whoever is contesting our sameness is sure heading for doom.
Whoever is contesting our sameness is in shambles
Whoever is contesting our sameness may be ashamed
Whoever is contesting our sameness might be insane.

1

VAGINA
ANATOMY

CHAPTER 1

VAGINA HOMOGENEITY

Vagina definitions available in the public domain and from anatomists:

The vagina is an elastic, muscular tube connecting the cervix of the uterus to the vulva and exterior of the body. It is located in the pelvic body cavity posterior to the urinary bladder and anterior to the rectum, measuring around three inches in length and less than an inch in diameter. The vagina stretches to become several inches longer and many inches wider during sexual intercourse and childbirth. The inner surface of the vagina is folded to provide greater elasticity and to increase friction during sexual intercourse. The vagina lining is pinkish red throughout.

Another definition goes thus; vagina is a fibro muscular elastic tubular tract which is a sex organ. The reddish pink passage leads from the opening of the vulva to the uterus, but the vaginal tract ends at the cervix. The vagina is an elastic muscular canal that extends from the cervix to the vulva, the internal lining of the vagina consists of stratified squamous epithelium. Beneath this lining is a layer of smooth muscles which may contract during sexual intercourse, beneath the muscle is a layer of connective tissue called adventitia which is six to seven and the half [6 to 7.5cm] or two and the half to three inches [2.5 to 3 inches] across the anterior wall front and 9cm [3.5 inches] across the posterior fornix deeper than anterior. During sexual arousal, the vagina expands in length and width. Its elasticity allows it to stretch during sexual intercourse and during child bearing. The vagina together with the inside of the vulva is reddish pink in colour.

The vagina is an elastic, muscular canal with a soft, flexible lining that provides lubrication and sensation. The lining of a vagina is pinkish red in color. The vagina connects the uterus to the outside world. The vulva and labia form the entrance, and the cervix of the uterus protrudes into the vagina forming the interior end. The vagina is the functional organ of the female reproductive organ system. It extends from the vulva externally to the uterine cervix internally and is located within the pelvis, anterior to the rectum and posterior to the urinary bladder. It has a pinkish red lining shade. It lies at 90 degrees angle in relation to the uterus and is held in place by endopelvic fascia and ligaments. It is a potential space that is easily distended.

The word vagina is from the latin v~agina, which literally means 'sheath' or scabbard, it is a fibro muscular elastic tubular tract which is a sex organ, the pinkish red passage leads from the opening of the vulva to the uterus but the vaginal tract ends at the cervix.

2

HOMOGENEOUS AND NOT HETEROGENEOUS

CHAPTER 2

═══════════════

HOMOGENEOUS
AND NOT
HETEROGENEOUS

The reason why the real properties of vagina were discussed earlier was because of the false belief in the adage that "varieties are the spice of life" and that applies to the vagina as well, but this cannot be in the case of vagina. Vagina is homogeneous. The "homogeneous commodities" possessors may be different in personality, but what they carry are the same, the "commodities" are not heterogeneous, so the excuse for the involvement with many "possessors" is not tenable. No matter the color or the race, the "commodity" is homogeneous; the "commodity" is the same world over. It is understandable if there are mad rush for heterogeneous commodities because they are not the same, they are different and not serving the same purpose. But a situation where there is a mad rush for a homogeneous commodity by an individual is strange. The "commodity" that is turning the world upside down is "homogeneous" not heterogeneous.

Homogeneous commodities are items whose parts and elements are all of the same kind and nature, having the same degree or dimensions all through in every term. The main striking property of homogeneous commodities are their uniform composition, (when something is said to be uniformed; they are said to be of the same texture, type, nature, and form).

5

They are also said to be uniformed in character in the way they work, and the way they are activated. Their behavioral patterns are the same, they act in the same manner, their response to stimuli are the same.

Synonyms of homogeneous are: EQUIVALENT, MATCHING, KINDRED, SIMILAR, SAME, CONGRUENT, IDENTICAL, LIKE, EXACT, COGNATE, COMPARABLE, AKIN AND ANALOGOUS.

EQUIVALENT: Means something that has the same value, purpose, and job as something else.

MATCHING: Being the same with the other thing.

KINDRED: It belongs to the same group or specie.

SIMILAR: Items are like the same, look alike.

SAME: Things are exactly like each other.

CONGRUENT: Means an item is technically the same size and shape.

IDENTICAL: Things that are exactly like each other

LIKE: To resemble something

EXACT: To be exact is to be a carbon copy.

COGNATE: A word in one land that has the same origin as a word in another language

COMPARABLE: Similar to something else in number and quality.

AKIN: Similar to an item

ANALOGOUS: Composed of parts or elements that are all of the same kind not heterogeneous, having a common property throughout.

The common word for most of the synonyms is the word "same" which also implies uniformity.

All over the world, from Asia to Africa, from Africa to Europe, from Europe to Australia, from Australia to Antarctica, from Antarctica to North America, from North America to South America, there is uniformity in their descriptions of vagina, ironically each of them gave their personal descriptions without resorting to the other. Its homogeneous properties are attested to by all the anatomists around the world. In fact, seven continents of the world attestation cannot really be faulted.

In a nutshell, vagina is indeed a homogeneous commodity or a homogeneous item the world over.

Heterogeneous on its side is an item that consists of dissimilar or diverse ingredients or constituents. It is also referred to as any commodity that is not uniformed in structure or composition, diverse in character and content. They are visibly consisting of different components, and elements that are not of the same kind of nature and their functions are totally different.

If a heterogeneous commodity is causing any fuss in the society, it is understandable because every human being loves to have a taste of different things, then the adage "variety is the spice of life" can now be relevant, but not in the case of a homogeneous commodity.

Synonyms of heterogeneous are: DIVERSE, VARIED, VARYING, VARIETY, VARIEGATED, MISCELLANEOUS, ASSORTED, MIXED, SUNDRY, DISPARATE, MULTIFARIOUS, DIFFERENT, DIFFERING, MOTLEY AND PATCHWORK.

DIVERSE: To be very different from each other.

VARIED: Consisting of many different kinds of things or people.

VARIEGATED: Having different color marks on it.

VARYING: Different from each other.

MISCELLANEOUS: Set of many different things or people who do not seem to be connected with each other.

ASSORTED: Various different types

MIXED: Consisting of several different types of things or people.

SUNDRY: Not similar enough to form a group.

DISPARATE: Consisting of things or people that are very different and not related to each other.

MULTIFARIOUS: Items of many different kinds.

DIFFERENT: Dissimilar, not like something or someone else.

DIFFERING: To be different from something in some way. Having opposite opinions.

MOTLEY: A group of people or things that are very different from each other and do not seem to belong together.

PATCHWORK: Something that is made up of a lot of different things.

The common words for heterogeneous synonyms are "different" and "dissimilar". If it is different or dissimilar, then it is not vagina because from all indications the "commodity" is homogeneous.

If it is attested to of being homogeneous, then the demand for more than one at a time is absurd, especially when possessing more than one legitimately can bring about a total destruction of a life time career, labour, sweat, achievement, honour, fortune, dignity, self -esteem and can even lead to the wiping out of a whole lineage.

It is an acceptable norm in a decent society if you have multiples of heterogeneous products because they are different and the usages are not the same, they are dissimilar, but when you possess a multiple of a homogeneous product, then there is a cause for alarm.

A commodity that is not scarce, an identical item, a homogeneous product should not be turned into an altar where genius becomes dullard, fortunes are sacrificed, destinies are maimed, honour becomes horror, dignity becomes disgrace, where shame is turned into a bath water, destiny becomes like a shale, and brilliant careers are pulverized. All things being equal there shouldn't be any reason for an item that is homogeneous in nature to cause catastrophe. He who is completely besotted by the "homogeneous commodity" is doomed for life.

The abysmal ignorance on the part of the victims as to the true properties of what is causing wanton destruction to lives, careers, and fortunes are breathtaking.

The number one property and fact is that the "commodity" in question is homogeneous, product A, B, C and product D to Z are the same, they are not two sides of a coin; they are identical products serving the same purpose. The number two fact to assimilate is that it is not the "commodity" that is giving you different feelings, it is your own personal sensual feeling or reactions which are created or formed by you and not the "commodity" that is making you feel different and thinking that the "commodity" is not homogeneous! You are the major determinant factor on how your feelings react to stimuli. It is what your sensory organ sends to your brain that reflects your emotions and actions.

Your mind and emotions are sending false information into your brain making you believe a lie that the "commodities" are not homogeneous because of your feelings at diverse encounters. Folks, this disconnect and the lies are set to pulverize your destiny.

Your thoughts create your feelings, actions and reactions, it is not the "homogeneous commodity" that determines how you feel after and during an encounter; it is your thoughts and you are the controller of it. It is what you send to your brain that you experience and manifest, if your thought refuse to see sexual escapade as an enjoyment, you won't see it as one, so it is not the "commodity" that is bringing you the enjoyment, you are the one creating one by your thought. You are the product of your thoughts. You determine what gives you pleasure and not the other way round.

Let's take everyday happenings around us as a case study.

Have you observed a situation where two people of the same age, stature and carriage were both given ten strokes of cane by the same person and on the same palm with the same strength, one burst out in laughter while the other one burst out crying like a baby, was it the cane that treated them differently? Of course not, one actually made up his mind not to cry and this signal has been sent to his brain and the other has programmed his mind and brain to the contrary. Would you now say that it is the cane that determined whether one will cry and the other party will burst out in laughter? It was what their minds sent to their senses that are being manifested physically, it has nothing to do with the cane.

3

HOMOGENEITY

CHAPTER 3

HOMOGENEITY

Homogeneity is the state of a product, commodity, object or an item being homogeneous. This is said to be the same, identical, similar or essentially alike. The vagina, the way it is structured in women anatomy is just the same with Lady A, B, C to Z. The Master Architect, structured the master piece in such a way that there cannot be any confusion in selection of one above the other, he envisaged there might be problem of choice in his absence which will not augur well for the society and mankind, so he made sure they are homogeneous, the placement of clitoris in black race is the same with that of white race and with people of mixed race, he saw to it that the placement of fibro muscular elastic tubular tract is on the same spot in the seven continents of the world namely Asia, Europe, Africa, North America, South America, Australia and Antarctica. The positioning of labia in Dubai is the same as in Canada and Ethiopia. The fixing of adventitia in the U.S.A is the same in Nigeria, China, Brunei, Togo and Dublin. The carving out of the elastic in the vagina in Liverpool, New York, Ireland, Shanghai, Bombay and Cotonou is the same way it was carved in Afghanistan, Saudi Arab and in the suburbs of Turkey and Iran. The vulva was just fixed at the same corner in Indonesia, Japan, Kuwait, Gambia, Korea, Georgia, Cape Verde, Netherlands and United kingdom. so also the placement of cervix to the vulva.

The Master Architect knew that if they are identical or essentially alike, it will put an end to the crisis that might resort from choice, he knew if he makes everything homogeneous having one is having all, there will be no problem of choice, once you pick one it is the same with the one your neighbor picked and covetousness is out of the game.

He knew the "commodity" has to be homogeneous in order to have sanity in the society, because if the "commodity" is heterogeneous there is bound to be greed and anarchy, you cannot stop people from having as many different things as they love to have because such items are not serving the same purpose and are not the same thing. It is like telling people that if they own a house, they cannot own a car, if they own a car, they cannot own a television, these instructions cannot be possible because all those items are not related in any way, they are not serving the same purpose and are not the same thing at all.

And in nailing the confusion that might resort from choice finally to the wall, He made sure the "commodity" lining has a universal color and shade for the whites, the blacks and people of mixed race from the continents of Asia to Africa, South America, North America, Europe, Antarctica, and Australia. He made it undisputable striking PINKISH RED.

4

THE
MIRAGE

CHAPTER 4

THE MIRAGE

It is a rain, I say it is not a rain. It is a rain water I say it is not a rain water. But I can see it, can't you see what I'm seeing, no what you are seeing is not a rain water, what you are seeing is an optical reflection they call it mirage. No it is not an optical reflection of any kind when we get to the front you will see it is a rain water.

I'm having fun and enjoying myself, oh the pleasure is breathtaking! I say that is not enjoyment and it cannot be, the action that will prey on your very life and destroy a colorful destiny cannot be enjoyment. It is a mirage, it is an illusion, you have slipped into deception, and your reasoning is clouded. Never be deceived that you were having pleasure in illegal entanglement with "homogeneous commodities", that it is just sex, it is not just sex it is a covenant you are enacting. Don't be deceived sexual activities are covenant practices. There shouldn't be any big deal over a "homogeneous commodity" that is not scarce whoever is led astray by it is not wise. It is the same throughout, no variety, your feelings are deceiving you that they are different. You have fallen into the deception of thinking that the optical reflection on the expressway is rain water. The truth about "homogeneous commodities" is accruing one is accruing all.

Go and buy four units of 2010 Camry cars brand at the same time for your personal use and see how people will rate you, of course the first thing that comes to people's mind is that you need to have your head examined, your action will raise many questions on your state of mind.

We are in a world awash in love stories, most of them are lies, they are not love stories at all they are lust stories, sex fantasy and sodomy domination stories. From the cradle we are fed on lies about love bothering on varieties and free will in a free world that has nailed many colorful destinies and careers. We have a hard time understanding the fundamental ingredients of our daily actions, our minds and imaginations are crippled with lies about love. "I'm in love is what readily comes to our mind and mouth when there is a crush with a possessor of "homogeneous commodity" where as in actual fact we are in lust, illusion has taken over our reasoning faculties, but the beauty of human nature is that we all have our sober moments and the way we are wired especially the conscience is that no matter the façade whoever is sinking knows that he's sinking.

A promising career and future shouldn't be slaughter on the altar of a product that is not scarce and the same thing the world over.

Do not be deceived, there is no vagina that is laden with diamond neither is anyone laden with gold dust or a silver plated one, they are all homogeneous. If fortune is what you are searching for by entangling yourself, the honourable way out is through personal hard work and diligence.

"Son you are heading on a suicide mission with all your sexual escapades" declared sixty eight year old father, Prince Daniel in an audible tone. "Dad it is not what you think, it is not about sex at all, it is just the beauty, the charm and their kind gestures, that is the magnetic forces". "I see, no problem if that is what you saw and liked about them, since you have a "homogeneous commodity" in the house already you can keep them and be relishing yourself with their beauty and charms alone, since it is not what i think". "Let's strike a deal son just keep them and be beholding their beauty without going into them, since it is not what I think". Declared the old man.

It is the package not the 'product' declared Anthony, I chose to disagree it is the 'product' not the package, if it is not the 'product' as you are contesting then acquire the package and not tamper with the 'product' and the whole world will be at peace. It couldn't have being the packaging that is the attraction at all if it the packaging, a king will not abandon his well adorned queen, gracefully dressed in the palace to go searching for the ladies of the night whom he could hardly recognized after an encounter. If it is the packaging and not the 'product' the head of a corporation will not abandon an equally intelligent madam to dig it out with the cleaner. If it is the packaging and not the 'product' a political rival will not use the 'weapon' to take away the dominion of a rival. If it is the packaging and not the 'product' why will an aristocrat descend so low to rub shoulder with a plebeian.

The truth of the matter is that it is the 'product' not the packaging because if the 'product' is not forth coming the packaging becomes less attractive. Wisdom dictates you steer clear of a 'product' that destroys destinies with ease, it is not worth the while to tamper with a 'product' that is not yours which can take away your very being and cut short your purchasing power in the market place and committee of men.

When you slipped into the delusion of sexual enjoyment don't ever let anybody deceive you about the option of applying discipline as the only way out because a spiritual transaction has been set in motion in your body and your heavens. An edge has been broken.

Vagina Homogeneity

Don't be deceived that you are having pleasure in illicit amorous activities, your entanglement is a covenant activity, it is a contract, you have ignorantly signed a deed of agreement you are not likely to fulfill or bargained for, which the other party can use against you at any time. An agreement you don't even know the terms and conditions of before appending your signature. Ignorance is no mistake in law!

5

"OPPORTUNITY COST"

CHAPTER 5

"OPPORTUNITY COST"

M ultiple definitions of opportunity abound all over, but one thing that is constant to all is that it ALLOWS the execution of an action, palatable or otherwise. Being positive or negative now depends on the individual volition.

Opportunity is a chance to do what you have loved to do, opportunity is an occasion when it is easy for someone to do something, and it is also the creation of an avenue to satisfy ones sensual pleasure.

Opportunity is also referred to as a chance to satisfy one's intention and an open door to satisfy a craving.

So, opportunity is a situation that creates an enabling environment for the actor, it might be to do well or to do badly.

It might be to save life or to commit murder; it might be to commit adultery or to work away from it.

"Oh, I had a chance to caress my secretary's boobs when every other member of staff had gone on break".

"Oh, I had a chance to escape my secretary's overtures when we were alone in the office and somebody just knocked at the door!"

In both analogies, one thing that was common to both actors were their abilities to achieve their aims; they felt good by their actions. They were both contented with their achievements, but their circumstances were different.

It is obvious from all these definitions that it is a good thing, it is a plus to the beneficiary irrespective of how it was used (negatively or positively), the bottom line is that the actor is able to satisfy his sensual gratification. Short and sharp, a craving is satisfied. To the actor, it is a plus, an achievement, an advantage, or a benefit.

"I feel real good, it was a great opportunity to shower back the love she shown toward my mummy."

"At last, the opportunity came for me in the midnight to avenge my sister's death without anybody tracing the murder to me".

From the above analogies, all opportunities are good, beneficial and a plus at least from the point of view of the actor. Every opportunity you encounter in life is either to make you or mar you, depending on how you handle it.

Cost at its other end is a minus; it means something you have to pay to get an item.

Cost is the amount of money that you pay in ordering a commodity; it is also the money you use in buying something.

Cost is a value you give for something.

In a nutshell, cost is a minus to an individual involved in a transaction; it takes something out of the buyer after something has been delivered!

A cost is a payment.

A cost reduces you.

A cost can be considered as a penalty.

Cost can be an investment.

Cost is what you lose in exchange for something.

Cost is something you damage to achieve something.

Cost is what is given away to achieve something.

Cost is the opposite of benefit, which means cost is a disadvantage.

Cost is costs, price, charge, fee, and fare, so it is a reduction all the way, a minus.

Common sense demands that cost must be commensurate with the returns, otherwise you are running at a loss. In our normal daily activities, if we buy anything that people felt was overpriced they will declare that we have been cheated! So, any venture that does not worth the kind of effort we put into it, is a bad venture people will declare.

Why would the economist then bring in something that is a plus and combine it with a minus in forming the term opportunity cost? I will jokingly answer the question on their behalf in order to defend my own piece, everything that must be of benefit to you or a plus in your life [either good or bad] must definitely cost you something, that is taking something out of your life, you cannot have your cake and eat it. As the opportunity is dropping something into your life because it is a plus, the cost is taking something out of your life because it is a minus.

The cost must surely take something out of your life; it may be strength, honour, dignity, or elevation.

Opportunity to fornicate comes into your life and brings in the cost of shame.

Opportunity to commit adultery comes into your life and brings in the cost of disgrace.

Opportunity to engage in illicit amorous relationship with a possessor of "homogeneous commodity" comes into your life and brings in the cost of public disgrace.

Opportunity to lie comes your way and brings in the cost of embarrassment.

Opportunity to steal comes your way and carries the cost of humiliation.

Opportunity to commit murder comes into your life and carries the cost of death with it.

Opportunity to usurp comes into your life with the cost of humbling demotion.

Opportunity of greed comes into your life and brings in the cost of lack and penury.

An economist will define opportunity cost of a choice as the value of the best alternative forgone.

It is also the cost of missed opportunity, it is the opposite of the benefit that would have been gained had an action not taken or been. A benefit, profit, or value of something that must be given up to acquire or achieve something else.

Opportunity cost is the process of choosing one good or service over another.

With all these economists definitions, it still boils down to the fact that something is lost to gain something. The ball is in your court to decide what is expedient to lose in order to gain the other.

6

AN
IMAGE
OF
GOD

CHAPTER 6

AN IMAGE OF GOD

The book of the beginning says 'let us make man in our image, in our likeness'-[Gen 1:26]

You are made in the image and the likeness of God, this simply implies that everyman is made after God's likeness. Men are made in the image of God, to be made in the image of something means you are a carbon copy of that person, so in a nutshell you are God's look alike, you are the same with the personality you are carrying His likeness.

If the author of life say let us make man in the image of a goat or a dog or a hen that automatically means we'll be carrying the likeness of those animals and manifest their conducts, but He bestows on us such a great privilege to carry His image and be in His likeness. What a great privilege to have such a status!

The outcome of this privilege is that if God is a honourable God, we too must be honourable men because we carry His posture. If you are to remain a honourable man God has created you to be, then you have a role to play, for every privilege, there is always a part to be played by whosoever the privilege is bestowed on and your part is not to dishonour yourself.

If you want to remain a honourable man that God has made you from creation then you don't dishonour your body by illicit entanglement with a "homogeneous commodity" when you possess one already or you can possess one legitimately if you so desired.

You need to know that every other sins you commit are outside your bodies, the only sin on the surface of the earth that you commit against your body and your personal self is a sexual sin. So, why must you be wicked to yourself? If you want to be cruel at all, must it be to yourself?

No right thinking person will take a knife and start cutting his body or carry acid and pour it on his body for any reason on the surface of the earth. You and I know that anybody that does this needs a medical attention, even without him calling for help, we will be the ones that will cry out on his behalf and call the attention of people in authority to the strange behaviour and a rescue team is constituted to help the person.

A mad man would not even do such to himself, he will rather do that to another person, or have you ever seen a mad man attacking himself or pouring acid on his own body? If you have seen one, that would have been on a rare occasion because I have never seen one, but I have seen a mad man attacking passers- by on several occasions. Insane people feel pains too, so they seldom attack themselves; they rather inflict pains on other people. Do you know that by engaging in an illicit amorous relationship you are cutting yourself with knives and pouring acid on your body so as to destroy it and terminate your very life which you and I know that even an insane person will not do to himself. Why have you chosen to be cruel to yourself? Why must you dishonour yourself in an illicit relationship with a "homogeneous commodity possessor"? Why must you with all your education and exposure if not under a spell take a knife and cut yourself? What if you cut your veins in the process and bleed to death or mistakenly pour the acid on your eyes and you lose your sights? Think deeply about your actions, I'm sure you won't want to injure your body even if you are a mad man.

"Flee from sexual immorality, all other sins a man commits are outside his body, but he who sins sexually sins against his own body" [1Cor.6 :18]

Have you ever seen a mad man dancing naked in the market place? If you have seen one, I'm sure you won't want to be in his shoes, you won't even envy him, but that is exactly what you are doing when you engage in illicit amorous relationships. The only permitted situation where a man and woman are naked before each other and do not suffer or experience any form of shame either psychologically or emotionally is in a marriage situation. No shame, no guilt and no crushed self-esteem.

"The man and HIS WIFE were both naked and they felt no shame" Gen 2: 25

Note here, the man and HIS WIFE, not the man and the girl, not the man and the woman, not the man and the lady, not the man and the queen, not the man and the princess, not the man and the madam nor was it the man and the babe.

You are made in the image and the likeness of God, shame and disgrace are not supposed to be your portion and if you play your own part well as a honourable man, it will not.

"A body destined for resurrection should not be used for immorality".

Cooperate with your maker and live a honourable life, because that is your birth right in the first place.

"My legs are aching" anybody can declare that anyhow, anywhere, because we all believe that there is no big deal about it, "my vagina is aching" grave silence will rend the atmosphere and everybody will blush and consider the person saying this as being crazy; in fact, people will avoid such a one as a plague because they felt the utterance was out of place. Why such a reaction over such utterance? Because we know and believe vagina is sacred. If all and sundry held such a strong belief that vagina is sacred, why are we defiling it? Why are you treating a sacred thing in an unholy manner? Why will you abuse what is sacred?

7

THE WANNABE SYNDROME

CHAPTER 7

THE WANNABE SYNDROME

A man's dignity is in being who you are and who you are is in being your real self, being your real self is in being true to yourself, being true to yourself is in being true to your maker. Never at any point in your life try to be like that other guy, who knows whether that other guy is trying to be somebody else.

The Wannabe syndrome is a phenomenal that has drown so many lives and destroyed so many destinies. Wanna bes are people who are not sure of themselves they always want to be somebody else.

Dave the country director of the largest telecom corporation in his country was always in blue striped designer shirt, "oh that is the big boys colour, so anytime I want to go shopping, I go for different types of designers blue striped shirts. That is the touch of affluence and class" declared Richy, he was ignorant of the fact that the striped blue shirts are the code sign of the male fraternity Dave belongs to!

Greg is a happening guy and he is enjoying life to the fullest, so people around him felt. He has a bubbling career and abundant luxury, beautiful ladies are at his beck and call, "that's my man I want to be like that," says Flot. Oblivious of the fact that Greg is suffering from ancestral curses!

It is not because Greg has a great career or swimming in abundant luxury that babes are flocking around him, even if Greg was to be a pauper, babes will always be flocking around him like bees. Greg's grandfather was the poor of the poor, he had the same issue, Greg's father died in penury, he had the same problem, what is causing Greg secret tears is the attraction Flot is dying for, he wanted to be the ladies man in the society, he wanted to be just like Greg while Greg was dying to be a better and more honourable man.

Your inability to be true to your self is what has landed you in the present predicament, a real strange island, but what can you do with your eyes wide opened you have traded your identity. A strange toiling in search of an identity that was not lost in the first place. How does one search for something that is not lost other than to embark on an endless toiling that will prey on his very life and destiny? The Greg that you thought was the hottest guy in town is weeping aloud, silently looking for a way out.

The endless search for a "homogeneous commodity" that you already have will surely drain you, your finances, blood, self esteem and your relevance will deplete and very soon your very structure will dilapidate.

Quest for relevance is landing you where you don't want to be. The irony of life is that by the time you land there you know for sure this is not where you want to be. In your sober moment, you will ask yourself "HOW DID I GET TO THIS IN THE FIRST PLACE"! But the damage has been done already, there is a crack in your water pitcher, a broken egg cannot be gathered back into a shell, 'araldite' or super glue cannot perform the wonders.

8

SUPERLATIVE
MAGNETIC
TURNOVERS

CHAPTER 8

SUPERLATIVE MAGNETIC TURNOVERS

"We have had a superlative year, we've never had it so good since inception, we were able to exceed the targeted turnover with over a thousand percent increase, we have every cause to celebrate this financial year end in a spectacular way" declared Mr Osei Tutu, the managing director of OST corporation at a roundtable board meeting.

Mr Acheampong declared: "let us take a special stock to know what was responsible for this laudable achievement as to leverage on it in the coming year". The Managing Director cuts in, in his usual baritone voice, "didn't you observe what has been happening in the past twelve months, it was when I started dining with the country's President and the opinion leaders that the company's fortune took a new turn for the better. This relationships changed the volume and level of our clienteles. Its magnets people of value to us, the magnetic attraction from people of timber and caliber we now enjoy was what brought about the company's turnaround". He burst out in an uppity laughter, the kind that reflects the state of mind of a man of affluence who is living a debt free life and doesn't need to quiver at the presence of his bankers. "This is what we call SUPERLATIVE MAGNETIC TURNOVER, my association with Mr President and his likes has attracted a lot of successful people and goodwill to me and the corporation", he emphasised. "Likes attract likes, you call it law of attraction if you like", and he stood up with his glass of champagne and exited the boardroom without an excuse and dashed to the parking lot.

The way high- end relationships attract fortune to Mr Osei Tutu and his corporation is the same way illicit amorous relationships attract it's stock in trade to you. Illicit "homogeneous commodities" will magnet lies, theft, shame, and every other vices you can think of into your lives.

Before you know it, you just discover that you are now a pathological liar, because you have to cover up your tracks. You found out you have started stealing, embezzling funds put in your care, changing figures at random in order to maintain your new lifestyle, because the strange island you have landed yourself is money consuming. It will be like servicing a debt when you don't have money to offset the principal. Your integrity is gone in the process, your YES becomes NO and your NO becomes YES.

Impatience becomes your way of life, you want to do things in a hurry not because that is your nature, but you have to put up a front to keep people who are likely to question your new lifestyle at bay or you become so quiet and patient as to confuse people of your real identity and escapades. Confusion crept into your life with easy because your heaven is scrambled up.

Is it the numerous strange ailments that will creep into your body that we want to discuss or the needless spiritual problems and battles you have to fight?

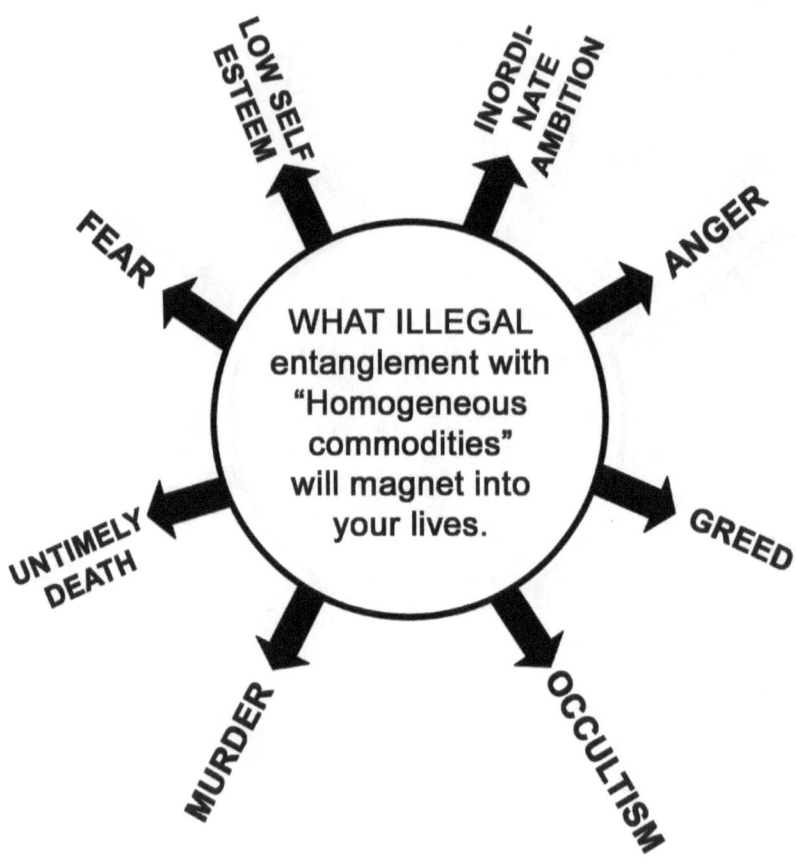

9

"COMMISSIONS ON TURNOVERS"

CHAPTER 9

"COMMISSIONS ON TURNOVERS"

The experience after numerous ugly turnovers traceable to illegal entanglement with "homogeneous commodities" are overwhelming, those turnovers also attracts their own commissions that permeate ones total being from the spiritual to the physical states. Ones spirit, soul and body must definitely share out of the burden caused by the body [flesh].

The commission on turnovers are always charged in form of bankruptcy [financial mess], money that is hitherto abundant in your hands suddenly becomes scarce, it is always one form of unforeseen expenditure or the other, you are always broke even if you have the keys to the Central bank vault you will still not have enough, insufficiency becomes a common place in your life.

Another commission on turnover that is traceable to all that are entangled is frequent and consistent nightmares in form of bad and violent dreams, meaningless dreams, finding oneself at dreaded events and where one is not suppose to be in the sleep.

Traumatic and extremely frightening experience becomes a familiar night time occurrence. It is always the dreams of rising and falling, struggling in climbing a hill, rock or ladder. Toiling and fighting one battle or the other in the sleep becomes a common place.

Confusion becomes a part and parcel of you. This kind of confusion is not the type that will make you call colour purple colour red but it is the kind of confusion that will make you refute a statement of truth that is truly stated, which is obvious to everyone around you that it is the truth. It is not a physical confusion of not knowing where to turn to when you approach a 'T' junction, but a spiritual confusion of not accepting the "gospel truth" over most issues, and this is a very delicate and dangerous state any human being can found him or herself.

Sound judgments become a luxury in ones life, ability to act decisively and promptly over urgent issues become a herculean task for you. Irrational decisions come easily to you, you make senseless and barbaric decisions you cannot even explain yourself.

Vulnerability to sickness and diseases such as weakness and in explainable tiredness, high blood pressure, excruciating body pains at diverse times, sexually transmitted diseases and brain block become part of you.

Some of the commissions the turnovers attract are also lack of boldness, high service becomes your way of life, you become an easy prey when destruction is lurking at a corner you will be the last person to discern it, you walk easily into traps and set ups. You fall into one enslavement or the other, you are in a state of being dominated and manipulated against your will.

The only "vocation" that attacks every facet of your being. Spirit, soul and body. Your spiritual state is leveled, non- physical aspect of your person like consciousness, thought, feeling and will are leveled, your physical body and structure also leveled. It makes it's marks on your spirit, soul and body without necessary asking your permission, it is an "interference" that does not know its boundary. It is invited to come and service your sensual gratification only, but before you know what is happening it has spread like cancer cells into other departments of your life that it was not invited into. [spirit and soul]. On the long run every part of your being is chipping out certain amount of commission on turnover at diverse time, if it is not sickness and diseases, it is financial mess or endless spiritual battles.

10

"COST OF PRODUCTION"

CHAPTER 10

"COST OF PRODUCTION"

Brilliant Andrew Hanson grew up in the suburb of Mississippi in the United States of America, the fourth born in the family of seven. A very sharp lad from a humble background, the family hardly takes three square meals in a day. Andrew's father works as an assistant in an automobile workshop in their neighbourhood and the mother in a farm settlement very close to the family house on part time basis.

The family income was relatively small to cater for the family of nine; none of the seven children could afford the luxury of an elementary education. The reality on ground was what actually made their mother to take up part time job, so the days she's not at work she's teaching her kids at home to make up for the inability to attend a regular school due to finances. Any time the mother is at work, the children had to go to another nearby farm to help out because an idle mind is the devil's workshop. Their remuneration is through a barter arrangement, the farm gives out some harvested produce in exchange for their labour.

To say life was tough for this family was an understatement, but their parents were labouring day and night to at least give their children something that can help them to get to their next level. Light out for this family was always close to the midnight because they couldn't afford any gadget that could make household chores easier and faster. The hardship the household passed through on a daily basis was phenomenal! But out of the seven children [five boys, two girls] Andrew Hanson was exceptional, he was able to secure an admission into a high school ahead of his brothers, her mother reluctantly allowed him to seat for the entrance examination into a public high school with his brothers alas it was only Andrew that was admitted.

Where will the money needed to buy the few school needs come from were the thoughts on his parents' minds. The family approached the farm where the children had being helping out to secure permanent job for the other boys. So that the family can press for weekly wages for the boys instead of the barter arrangement which the owners of the farm consented to in order to help them, but the girls still help out on part time basis in order to still be bringing harvested produce home so that there could be food on the family's table.

Through this arrangement Andrew's three brothers became farm labourers and he was able to make it through high school gallantly. Andrew secured an admission into a college of technology in Chicago, the whole family were happy, at least in about a couple of years Andrew will be done through school and secure a good job and probably relocate his whole family from the Mississippi suburb to Chicago, their expectations were high and to a certain extent sure because Andrew was a focused, compassionate and responsible guy, he would not bite the fingers that fed him, he appreciated all the prices every member of his family paid in sending him to school. The cost over Andrew's life was huge, financially and emotionally.

Like every other student in a city college, Andrew enjoyed his life to the fullest and faced his studies, he came out with a brilliant result and he was able to secure a well paid job in a computer firm on graduation. The success did not get into his head as everybody would have expected, he was still the old focused, compassionate, and responsible guy he used to be.

Good job, good remuneration, good family and peace of mind, Andrew was able to concentrate on his job, making exceptional contributions toward the progress of his company at diverse times and at the same time living his life to the fullest. Chicago night life was fantastic and Chicago babes were awesome! Andrew's lifestyle was a normal one for every guy of his status. He was not over doing things, he was moderate, and life is meant to be enjoyed. He got married two years into his employment at the computer company. Plans was on top gear to relocate his family to the city but not Chicago because he felt the city might be too expensive and fast for anybody that was not used to city life, so he was contemplating relocating them to Connecticut or Arizona and set his brothers up in the agricultural field which they have mastered through the years and also planned to set up a food processing outfit as a family business. A golden fish cannot be hidden, Andrew's company was planning to open a regional office in Dubai to cover the Asia interest of his corporation, from all indications Andrew was the most qualified and everybody in the organisation knew that his time has come, but alas! there are two other professional colleagues in his organisation that are from that region that are eyeing the same post.

The time has come for the corporation to send representatives to Dubai to do underground work to survey the environment, study the market terrain and meet with the opinion leaders in the region. The corporation president with other board members summoned Andrew Hanson and the two other guys from that region to a board meeting and gave them the mandate of all they were to do in Dubai for a period of twelve weeks and afterwards the office will take off. They admonished them to work as a team in order to take the organisation to a greater height.

Two days to their departure, the company's president invited Andrew Hanson to a morning tea meeting to inform him that after the opening of the Dubai regional office that the company planned to open an office in the United Kingdom and Andrew was going to manage the UK branch. So, he admonished him to do his possible best in giving the Dubai regional office assignment his best for a smooth take off, that the management would decide later which of the other guys to head the Dubai regional office.

America organisations value the place of marriage in their society, so Andrew Hanson left the shores of USA with his wife [Mrs Hanson took a leave of absence for four months from her employers] on the bill of the company. Fortunately, 80 percent of Andrew Hanson out of station allowance was paid to him before he left the USA, without taking a dime out of the money, he transferred the money to his people in Mississippi and their joy knew no boundary.

Dubai life was quite interesting but not as bubbling as Chicago city, Mr. and Mrs. Andrew Hanson loved their new temporary abode but for the harsh weather condition. Mrs. Hanson declared "darling I love this city but the weather is too hot". Andrew and the other colleagues got to work, surveying their new environment and espionage on other established brand in their field if need be. Business dinners, tea meetings, and golf clubbing outings became endless, which is normal for any business executive anyway.

Andrew and his team were doing their assignment as it should be done. There was no cause for Andrew to discuss what transpired at the tea meeting with the company's president two days to their departure with his colleagues. But the level of affluence and comfort they were exposed to in Dubai threw the two guys off balance, their imaginations started running riot, being the regional head in this beautiful city of affluence would not be a bad idea anyway. Oblivious of what was going on in their respective minds, the two guys started planning privately on how to eliminate Andrew and outshine one another. Andrew would not compromise standard, he cannot mismanage the company's funds at his disposal, neither will he sell out to other competitors and he's not a womanizer!

The first colleague Pnog by name introduced a marketing undergraduate in one of the country's university to Andrew at a golf course, after a lengthy discussion, the lady told Andrew that she wouldn't mind working as marketing executive for their company on graduation. The lady caught Andrew as an intelligent smart lady, with good diction and mastery of her terrain, having had her high school in Dubai, with being in her final year in the city university and a female golfer! Andrew penned down the lady's name as one of their proposed employees.

Pnog introduced the lady undergraduate to Andrew in good faith, although he was still thinking of how to pin Andrew down and get him out of his way. On a Saturday, Andrew took his wife with him to the golf club, on getting there; they met the lady undergraduate by the bar side, Andrew introduced the lady to his wife and told her all about their earlier discussion. Interestingly they got along well, in fact Andrew's wife and the lady left Andrew and his colleagues at the golf course to go shopping only to join them at the dinner later in the day.

Before anybody knew what was going on, Andrew and this lady have started an illicit affair. Only heavens knew what transpired between them. When Pnog got to know about the affair, he rebuked Andrew sternly and registered his disapproval over the development, he felt this can jeopardize the assignment they were in Dubai to execute and also affect his personal ambition. Pnog didn't see this as an opportunity to nail Andrew at all. His paramount ambition was on his mind to net the regional head job and he was not ready to allow any member of the team to be involved in any form of scandal that might make the management suspend their resolution in setting up a regional office in Dubai. Their third colleague got wind of what was going on in Andrew's private life a week to the completion of their assignment in Dubai, but not through Pnog. Pnog didn't discuss the issue with him and not with Andrew's wife, he was a gentleman, but never gave up his plans on nailing Andrew, but definitely not through that lady.

Andrew's third colleague can now breath a breathe of relief as he called Pnog that night to intimate him of what was going on in Andrew's life in order to nail him without letting Pnog know his real intention and motive. Pnog waved the issue aside and told his colleague that any other man could have done what Andrew did, that it was no big deal and the lady in question was single, more so Andrew's private life was not their business. Again, Pnog was afraid that if the head office got to know about this, they might recall the team with immediate effect and his ambition crushed.

But not with their third colleague who has seen an opportunity to cash on in Pnog's stance and disposition on the whole issue. He felt if having an affair with a single lady might not hold enough water before their employers, then planting a married woman on Andrew in an Arab territory in order to nail him would not be a bad idea and he would nail Pnog through his stance on the undergraduate lady's issue when he called his attention to what was going on in the team, which he deceptively felt could send a wrong signal in the new business territory they wanted to capture. Of course he recorded all the discussion he had with Pnog on the phone and sent spies after Andrew. He did this with perfection having discovered that Andrew cannot really rule his system, he planted a married woman on him promising to get the woman a plum job when he becomes the regional head and told the married woman about the other lady (undergraduate) in Andrew's life. He went to the extent of instigating the woman against the other lady in Andrew's life lying to her that Andrew has promised the lady undergraduate the same plum post he reserved for her. He told the woman to warm herself into Andrew's heart and bosom and get him all the necessary proofs of their affair which she did.

They arrived safely in the U.S.A after 12 weeks of tremendous work, with the team having a bill of perfect and enviable performance, a dinner was thrown for them. Their first day at work after their arrival from Dubai marked the day Andrew Hanson's world came crumbling down, with all the facts, lies and evidences tabled before the management staring Andrew Hanson in the face, the honourable man in Andrew Hanson took responsibility, threw in the towel even before investigation commenced. He was shown the way out, his world crumbled, hope dashed, and expectations cut off, not only his, but that of his extended family also. At 29, Andrew Hanson world melted like a vapor in his very presence.

The cost of producing Andrew Hanson was awesome and huge, every member of his family chipped in something, the labour, the struggle, the finances and numerous sacrifices all went with the winds! All his extended family dream of leaving Mississippi and having a new life suffered a major setback. Andrew Hanson heart ached for years and his shame could not be taken away. His wife though stood by him, but with an aching heart. A BRILLIANT CAREER SMASHED INTO PIECES WITHIN A TWINKLE OF AN EYE.

"I worked hard for all I have in order to give my children the best, I want them to have the best of everything", said Sir Agye Ladipo a former civil servant who abandoned his career in the civil service to pursue business because he felt being a salary earner could not fetch him the kind of money that was needed to give his children the best. He said "I am not ready to steal or change figures and my remuneration cannot maintain the kind of lifestyle I dreamt of. So I resigned at my middle age to pursue a vocation in buying and selling".

A family man to the core, Sir Ladipo was fortunate during his days to have won a government scholarship from high school through university. A product of the prestigious Imperial city university and a father of three often maintained that he would give his kids better education than he had, and he did exactly that. Kolapo his second son attended the best primary, secondary schools in Nigeria; afterwards, he was sent to Harwardite University where he graduated in flying colours. During Kolapo's years in school, he comes home every summer vacation and at Christmas time, (a good mummy's boy), a dream son of every family in a relationship with a medical doctor's daughter living down their street in Ikoyi, Lagos. Their relationship was steady and was known to every member of their families, but on platonic level. Getting to his final year in the university, he felt he was no more a small boy and he needed to take the relationship to the next level, he gave his girlfriend an engagement ring. One thing led to another, they indeed took their relationship to another level by sleeping together, promising to be faithful to each other. And Kolapo promised his babe marriage.

Dammy, Kolapo's senior brother got to know about this development and informed their parents who were first disappointed on hearing this, but later counselled them to face their studies and warned their son to be careful and stick to only one partner. "Women are all the same the world over son, so don't be deceived into tasting different varieties", counselled Sir Ladipo. Of course the father is a wise man, he knew what he was saying, he could not be talking about physical structure or complexion here.

Kolapo went back to school and his system changed, he started feeling lonely which was not the case before. He desperately wanted to get out of his strange feeling and he felt since he has promised his girl in Africa marriage, he could have flings with

49

other babes on campus before the summer vacation comes and he can travel home to be with his fiancée.

This was how Kolapo' s journey to the unknown started. After graduation, he came home to meet his fiancée, he could not just stay with her alone. He had chains of other girl friends as sleeping partners.

"Daddy was right after all when he said women are the same world over", Kolapo burst out after he had a fair share of ladies, the white, the black, and the people of mixed race, "I cannot just control my libido", he confided in his senior brother, Dammy. Kolapo got a good job in an oil company and his career was bursting forth, the parents were grateful to God and they were happy. He was very happy how fortune has smiled at him, good family background, solid education, exotic network of friends, abundant luxury, respect in the circle of family and friends, and a secured job, what else can a guy pray for? Kolapo had the same expectations as his father, he often told whoever cared to listen that he was going to give his children a better education than he had and shower them with the best things of life. True to his words and heart desires, he legitimately worked towards achieving this.

Sir Ladipo and his wife were couple that have penchant for hard work and the fear of God was paramount in their hearts. Noticing Kolapo' s systematic progress at work coupled with the gists he churns out on the happenings in the oil and gas sector, the parents picked interest in the field and planned to divest some of the family investments into oil and gas sector if the opportunity comes. Not too long, with the joint effort of the entire family and professional advice of Kolapo, they were able to float an oil and gas company that did well from inception which was being managed by both Dammy and Kolapo while still on salary job with the oil company.

Marriage bells would soon be ringing in the Ladipo's household, Kolapo informed his parents of his intention to take his long standing fiancée to the altar. The introduction was a beautiful one as both families were excited, the bride's family were happy and grateful to God that Kolapo did not dump their daughter after a long courtship for another babe, the Ladipos at their end too were proud of Kolapo for not embarrassing the family by bringing another woman to them and more also Kolapo was going to be the first family member that would be getting married, you can just imagine the joy of a closely knit family.

Another investment opportunity surfaced for the Ladipo's family, this time outside Nigeria in one African country. They won an oil block bid in that country and there was the need for Kolapo to give up his salary job to oversee the affairs of the new company with their foreign partners in Cape Verde. Cape Verde is a beautiful small oil rich island in West Africa.

All roads led to the island of Cape Verde to celebrate the feat, Sir Ladipo hired the services of a private airline to convey friends, family and business associates to the beautiful island, choice hotels were booked for all the guests on the Ladipo's bill, it was celebration galore throughout their four days stay.

Kolapo resumed in his new office and new environment with most of his colleagues being expatriates, life in Cape Verde was cool and pleasant, it's goodbye to Lagos hustling and bustling, for Kolapo, it was bye to Lagos stress and tension. To everybody's surprise Kolapo started falling ill, he was in and out of office for the first six months in his new station. The family felt probably it was due to change of environment and maybe because he was not used to the food in that country, so their most trusted cook was seconded to Cape Verde with a lot of Nigerian food to take good care of their precious son. The option of talking his fiancée to relocate to Cape Verde to take care of her man was out of it, the Ladipos were a very conservative and strict couple.

But Kolapo's health was still failing, but not at an alarming rate. He sought medical help abroad and he got better afterwards. Six months to his wedding, he started falling sick again, the father suggested that he should come home and rest, more so his wedding was around the corner. On his arrival in Nigeria, his proposed father in-law who happens to be a medical doctor suggested his hospital for a thorough medical checkup. The die was cast, the proposed father in-law got the greatest shocker of his life, he was devastated and ruffled, Kolapo has tested positive to human immunodeficiency virus(HIV). He could not manage the information as he broke the news to his wife before breaking the news to Kolapo and the Ladipos. One can understand his state of mind at that point in time, he was confused because his daughter was involved too, all hell was let loose at the in- law's resident which was just a stone throw from the Ladipos', accusations and counter accusations rent the air which invariably led to Kolapo 's fiancée fainting. In fact, the scene was a pitiable sight!

The entire Ladipos' household was thrown into confusion, they were shattered to their marrows, the shock was too much for them to take in, it was sorrow in their midst without death! The accusations and counter accusations between the two families took a new and dangerous turn, the Ladipos' didn't know how sexually involved their son was, but Dammy, their first born knew his brother has been quite sexually active to a large extent.

The Ladipos sought the help and the service of a counsellor in that field who was attending to Kolapo. He went back to work and his health was being managed, but his heart and that of his parents were broken, the agony of seeing their promising son dying in their hands was so much for them to bear.

Kolapo kept faith, he took it like a man, although he was now desperate to live than ever, his expectations in life were shattered, he wanted the hand of the clock to be turned back for him. He was desperate for a miracle!

Each passing day was a day of sorrow for the Ladipos, their hearts were bruised and they were really hurting, though they have extended families around coming very often to comfort them, but no one can really feel their pains with them. They held on to God showering their love on their ailing son, travelling to Cape Verde on a monthly basis to spend a couple of days with Kolapo.

Exactly 24 months after the deadly blow on the family, Sir Ladipo suffered a partial stroke which was being managed well. Ironically, unlike the father, the mother was able to keep faith for some years before she suffered acute depression. "My life is shattered", murmured Kolapo's mum. "Was it the nine months of carrying the pregnancy or the eighteen hours of delivery labour I passed through before I could have Kolapo that I want to think of or the hundreds of thousands of dollars we spent on sending Kolapo through school I need to talk about?", Kolapo's mum asked rhetorically.

The four-year ordeal Kolapo and his family passed through was like a torment of a hundred years, the cost of producing a brand like Kolapo was indeed gigantic and the production processes that went into producing Kolapo to say was huge was an understatement. After battling with depression for over two years, three months to his 34th birthday, Kolapo Ladipo passed on leaving his heart broken parents and siblings to mourn him.

Six months three days after Kolapo's passage, the mum who has been battling with acute depression died in her sleep. The circumstances of her son's death brought embarrassment to their household.

11

"RETURNS ON INVESTMENTS"

CHAPTER 11

"RETURNS ON INVESTMENTS"

Illegal entanglement with "homogeneous commodities" is the only investment in the whole world where returns on investments are not commensurate with the volumes of inputs at all. Numerous feasibility studies have revealed that the business is a high risk. In fact, according to international data nobody has ever break-even, not to talk of breaking through in the venture. [in the case of a normal business empire before an enterprise can be said to be making profits the company's revenue must be greater than their expenditure, that is their profit and loss account must reflect a larger figure in the profit column and lesser figure in the loss column. If the reflection is on the contrary, then the company is said to be running at a loss] But in this venture, in and out of season, the expenditure column is always far greater than the revenue column! "My own case is different, I'm going to employ the use of technology to outplay competitors and record a breakthrough", declared Richard. The inventors of the technology after a while declared they cannot guarantee one hundred percent success of their products and say abstinence is the best option, "Homogeneous commodities" monomaniacs beware!

"Good friends, follow your father's
good advice, don't wander off from
your mother's teachings.

Vagina Homogeneity

Wrap yourself in them from head to foot,
Wear them like a scarf around your neck.

Where ever you walk, they
Will guide you, wherever you go
they will guard you. When you
wake up, they will tell you what's next.

For sound advice is a beacon,
good teaching is a light,
moral discipline is a life path.
They will protect you from wanton women, from the seductive
talk
of some temptress, don't lustfully fantasize
on her beauty, nor be taken
in by her bedroom eyes.

You can buy an hour with a whore
for a loaf of bread, but a wanton woman
may well eat you alive.

Can you build a fire in your laps
and not burn your pants?
Can you walk barefooted on hot
coals and not get blisters?

It's the same when you have sex
with a woman that is not yours.
Touch her and you will pay for it.
No excuses, for a thief to steal when
He's caught he has to pay it back,
even if he has to put his whole house in hock.

Adultery is a brainless act,
soul destroying, self destructive.
Expect a bloody nose, a black eye

and a reputation ruined for good."
(Proverbs 6:20-33)

"A crown doesn't sleep outside the palace, all my children must stay under one roof; but the only thing I cannot tolerate is having two women under my roof at the same time because of my cosmopolitan lifestyle," says Prince Torey.

Mrs Torey has no objection since the prince is the "Alpha and Omega" in his household and together with her two sons welcome little Sandra and John; products of two different women into the house hold. Days after days, months after months they were happily living in Prince Torey's magnificent mansion in the Government Reservation Area, oblivious of the fact that prince first two sons have threatened poor little Sandra into submission and continuously abuse her sexually for years, but the principal culprit was Junior, the first son. By age 13, something tragic occurred in prince's household, it was discovered that Sandra was bleeding profusely from her private part and an abortion was detected. For almost a week before passing on, every attempt to know the culprit from Sandra fell on deaf ears as she refused to disclose the person that was responsible to her father and step mother, and the boys also feigned ignorance as to who could have been responsible. The Prince and his wife were quite shocked that such a thing could have happened under their roof, they were disturbed because they have grown to see Sandra as the princess of the house, they both made up their minds to get to the root of the matter. All their domestic staff both male and female were taken to the police station for interrogation, but they couldn't get a clue as to who was responsible. When it was the turn of the boys in the house [the three sons] the little information they got couldn't give the investigators any headway, the search went to Sandra's class teacher and the Mathematics teacher who happened to be males were invited for questioning, but no progress was made. "Sandra"s mum and maternal grand mum threatened fire and brimstone when another session of interrogations and investigation took place from her maternal side, but no tangible information that could give the investigation a boost was gotten.

The maternal grandmother insisted on unveiling the riddles behind her granddaughter's death. The woman told Prince Torey that she was going to hire the service of voodoo priest as to unveil the riddle, insisting that her 'Sandra' cannot die in vain. She wanted every member of Prince Torey's household to follow her to the shrine which Prince Torey vehemently objected to, but the woman was able to trick the domestic staff into appearing before the voodoo priest. She lied to them that the police would like to carry out another round of interrogation only for the staff to found themselves in a shrine, but they were all discharged by the priest. Before prince knew what was happening, the domestic staff resigned one after the other because the ordeal was becoming unbearable for them.

Prince Torey was accused by Sandra's grandmother of being the mastermind behind her granddaughter's ordeal and that he had to abort for the girl in order to cover up, that he defiled Sandra for ritual purposes, that was the reason the poor girl was not bold enough to let the cat out of the bag, and his vehement opposition on her taking the members of his household to the voodoo shrine was an indication that he was not innocent at all. Prince maintained his innocence and the grandmother stood her ground, the battle continued and this created a lot of tension within Prince Torey's household, there was no end to the case in sight and this ruffled prince's first son.

"I knew I slept with Sandra on a number of occasions, but I am still baffled as to how Sandra came across an abortion mixture or who actually gave her one. It couldn't have been me who was responsible for the pregnancy because I have not slept with her in the last six months," Prince's second son said.

"What do you mean by your statement? Are you now insinuating that I was responsible for her pregnancy and the abortion mixture?" Jnr, Prince's first son cuts in angrily and slammed the door against his brother.

Day in day out, Sandra's maternal grandmother made serious trouble with Torey's household and this gave Jnr sleepless nights. At this point he needed to create a distraction within the household that could douse the tension in the family and at the same time he needed to think fast in order to lose himself from the hook. With what his younger brother voiced out the other day, he knew beyond reasonable doubt that the guy had an idea of where Sandra's death might come from.

He carried out a systematic elimination of his younger brother through food poisoning, the sudden death of this boy indeed caused distraction from Sandra's saga and at the same time covered Jnr's track. This was how Torey's household lost two precious children within six months. Of course, the threats from Sandra's grandmother shriveled out and she was even accused of being the brain behind the boy's death in order to punish Prince Torey. Nobody had any cause to suspect any complicity from Jnr's end, Prince and his wife refused to be consoled.

For fear of what might happen to her son, John's mother, Prince Torey's last child came to pick her son.

Prince Torey and his wife picked up the pieces of their lives together and showered all their love on the only issue they were left with. Prince Torey became a loner, he was desperately looking for solution to what was happening at his home front, he needed help, he needed direction; but none came his way.

Jnr graduated from the university, on finishing his youth service, he travelled abroad for his master's degree and came back to the country after the two years sojourn. He got married to one of his colleagues in his work place, at least Prince and his wife experienced a new lease of life as another beautiful daughter was added to their family through marriage.

Jnr and his family were blessed with three children [two boys and a girl]. Most of the time, the grandchildren were with their grandparents and anytime they are on vacation, the whole family travels abroad. The Toreys were able to see light at the end of the tunnel, life was getting better and their wounds were healing gradually.

Conscience has not been fair on Jnr, guilt was eating him up day after day, years after years, the centre couldn't hold again; without earlier discussion with his wife, he sought audience with his parents and let the cat out of the bag and asked for their forgiveness. The parents couldn't believe what they were hearing, they felt Jnr was running crazy and sought the help of a psychiatrist, but the guy maintained his confession and insisted there was nothing wrong with him. The revelation was too much for the Toreys to take in, Prince Torey had a heart attack after two sleepless nights and died before help could come.

On hearing the confession without informing anybody, Jnr's wife abandoned him with the kids and relocated to Canada to start a new life.

The Bolong dynasty was an old one; it has been in existence for over a century. As they were flourishing in their sub region, so was their business empire, they were always adding province upon province every decade.

Lord Junpu has acquired ten provinces to his vast estate, solely for storage purposes. The family ship off loads every 45 days. They deal in articles of gold, silver and commodities.

The new acquired ten provinces were specially fenced and heavily guarded because of articles of trade that were stored there. Only six faithful guards who have been with the family over the years have access to the warehouse. So vast was the ten acquired provinces that they sat on eighty five hectares of land and the warehouse were divided into three, with each warehousing three different merchandise.

Lord Junpu commands so much influence in his province that there was no one that does not know him and he knew practically everyone in his provinces one on one. He has the milk of kindness flowing in his veins, he was the man of the people, always ready to listen and ever ready to help. So many community dwellers are living on his benevolence. He has helped so many enterprising people to get to their next level, his provinces was a flourishing one, both for him and all other dwellers. People always migrate from the neighbouring provinces to make the Bolong provinces their abode.

Sir Wang, a very enterprising man was one of the settlers in the province, but he still maintains his base at his native birthplace. He has a large expanse of land with a massive ten-storey structure just next door to Lord Junpu newly acquired 85 hectares of land warehouse housing his mistress Lady Shen, so beautiful was she that everybody in the province make reference to her beauty and the 'husband' knows this. He doesn't allow anybody to enter his compound in his absence unless the visitor is a female. All the domestic staff were females and they were well trained to handle tasks ordinarily meant for males.

Sir Wang being an itinerant business tycoon was hardly at home, although he has his wife in his native land, so the same way Sir Wang was not a regular face in his native land was also how he was at his high-rise edifice housing his mistress Lady Shen.

Lady Shen however has a lover by the name Yue in town who normally visits any time Sir Wang was not in town. Lady Shen sends the domestic staff on leave or give them offs anytime Yue is coming on visits. The Bolong dynasty was flourishing and everybody wants to associate with them, the influx of people into the business premises were getting out of hand, within six months of starting operations the place recorded up to seven burglary cases, three times they were able to apprehend those intruders to the warehouse, but before day break the culprits escaped, of course the number of the guards were relatively small to cover the place effectively so escapes were easy for the burglars.

Lord Junpu now gave his guards a command that whoever is caught should be beheaded, and the head be brought to him. His thought was that once he sees the head he would be able to recognise the personality and investigation within his provinces can lead to the arrest of all other accomplices for prosecution.

Lord Junpu wielded so much power and influence in his province, his words were laws, of course that was the easiest way to trace the syndicates, they cannot afford to arrest them alive, they don't want to leave anything to chances again, "who knows whether they are using mystical powers to effect their disappearances in the time past," declared Lord Junpu. The instruction was a secret one between Lord Junpu and the guards.

Sir Wang had gone on one of his numerous tours and he was expected back in three days, Lady Shen has sent for her lover to come and spend the night. It was not an offer Yue would reject or miss, he just fought his wife over a domestic issue, so he desperately needed a break from the house, he needed a breathing space and a petting palms. Unknowingly and unfortunately for those two lovers, Sir Wang had changed his mind on the trip and headed for the club where he cooled down till the wee hours of the day and later on headed home. The continuous bang on the gate made Lady Shen mad, just heading for the gate without a word for the guest she kept in the bedroom and even a word for the person at the other side of the gate at least to know the identity of the unwanted guest at the gate. She opened the gate in annoyance and got the greatest shock of her life, it was Sir Wang at the gate! Before he could query the whereabouts of the domestic staff at the gate, Lady Shen started shouting on top of her voice, "Xu, the master is around where are you, Xu the master is around where are you" at the same time leaving her 'husband' behind, racing towards the house. [Xu was the name of the lady security staff). The lover at his end got the message immediately, put himself together, back in his cloth at the speed of the light and jumped through the back window that oversees Lord Junpu warehouse as an escape route. "Bang bang" was the sound the warehouse guards heard, they raced towards the direction of the noise, caring less to verify the identity of the person before the count of three, Yue's head was on the ground of the warehouse.

At the day break the head was brought to Lord Junpu, lo and behold, the head was that of his son-in law, the embarrassment was too much for him, he couldn't carry on with the investigation as planned. Yue's wife who was Lord Junpu's only daughter was taken aback and shocked, she couldn't even fathom what has taken place, "is it possible for my husband to be the brain behind all the burglaries that has being taking place in the family warehouse and why on earth could he had descended so low? What has taken over him?". The extended family members were short of words, "what could have pushed Yue to engage in such a shameful act? Why has he chosen to steal from his father-in law knowing well that his wife is the man's only daughter and everything the man has belongs to them at his death?" The people of the province were equally shocked; tongues were wagging in the province, nobody could give a clue as to why Yue decided to steal from his wife's family. The guards too were shocked on knowing that it was Yue, Lord Junpu's son-in law that they had beheaded, they were afraid that Lord Junpu might ask for their own heads. The province was in disarray, only Lady Shen can give a clue to this mystery and she decided to keep quiet, and she did this forever and persuaded her lover for a change of environment which the man succumbed to. [There are so many mysteries connected to "homogeneous commodities" which cannot be traced or investigated properly, only heavens can unfold such mysteries to mortal men].

Lady Shen was fortunate, her escapade couldn't be detected, Yue was unfortunate, he couldn't live to tell the real story of what actually transpired and at the end soiling his family's name for what he did not do.

"My husband's priority is his family, he doesn't want me to work because he felt my staying at home taking care of the children and the home front is the best alternative in keeping the family," says Amina, a medical school graduate. She didn't object to the arrangement because her husband was a successful engineer who made more than enough to cater for the family and partially because she was lazy.

Within the first 12 years of their marriage, they have been blessed with nine lovely children, so theirs was a large comfortable family. By their thirteenth wedding anniversary, they moved into their fourteen bedroom duplex in a highbrow area of their state. Life was so comfortable for this family though their kids go to a good school in their vicinity, every summer, the engineer made sure they travel the world over on vacation.

A hardworking guy, before any of his colleagues could manage to build a house, he had built so many and had invested heavily in real estate in and out of his country, his vocation paved way for him as a structural engineer, as he's winning contracts to build for government and high-end individuals, he was building for himself on the side.

At age forty, he was called upon by his community to come and represent them in politics and he gladly obliged them. Engineer as he was always called by the wife, friends, family and colleagues began his political career. As an engineer and a contractor he had relationship and contacts with the politicians in his country, hence, the terrain was not new to him, in fact he was very happy and excited because he had the backing of his people and also an opportunity to make more money and wax more power and influence.

"Money without power makes one a good fellow, money combined with power is the real thing," Engineer declared in the midst of his friends at a club gathering. His community picked him because they felt he was the only one that has the financial might to represent them in politics, with his influence and wealth they could wrestle power from their opponents. Soon he got nominated as one of the governorship candidates of his party, the real politicking started. Money politics was the order of the day in his part of the world, if you don't have financial muscles and backings you cannot make any headway, in short money is politics and politics is money.

A shrewd businessman to the core, he believes politics is an investment, if you win, you will recoup your investment, if you don't, you align yourself with the winning camp in order to recoup the money that has gone down the drain and most importantly one should keep tap on his spending. So, in order to pursue his ambition for the primaries, he sold two of his houses and things actually worked out for him, he won the primaries and became his party's flag bearer.

The coast was now clear for him, his party was the most popular in his province as he had the full backing of his people and he was a moneybag, the only thing that was not working for him was that his people were really poor, they could not chip in a dime into his campaign funds. The other two opponents from other political parties could not match his force financially. One was a retired school principal, the other was a retired civil servant. Engineer was hundred percent sure that he was going to record a landslide victory, he went back to the drawing board to map out strategies on how to achieve this and how much he was going to expend on the project. As a shrewd businessman considering the caliber of his opponents, he pegged his campaign budget to certain minimum. He sold one of his three houses abroad to pursue his election expenses.

His circles of friends increased, both male and female, he courted the low and the mighty around and everybody knew he was going to win. But alas, one of the candidates died in a ghastly motor accident when returning from a campaign, the whole community was thrown into mourning the Engineer inclusive. But this could not upset the election and the campaign, it was just the party concerned that had to go back to the drawing board in order to pick a replacement as mandated by the electoral body.

After observing two days off campaigning in honour of the departed, Engineer continued with his campaign, moving from one village to the other, touring every nooks and crannies of his region, he was careful about his spending, "we are still within our budget", declared the engineer to some party faithfuls, every necessary hands had been "oiled" to their satisfaction.

The sudden death of their candidate gave the other party the opportunity to go back to the drawing board to shop for another candidate that could match Engineer money for money and power for power. They eventually got another son of the community who was equally up to the Engineer; the new candidate had spent quite a number of years abroad and had made so much money over there. After all the party's processes, the man's name was sent to the electoral body and he was confirmed as a replacement for the late aspirant.

The profile of the new aspirant ruffled the engineer to his marrow, his camp was thrown into confusion which necessitated the need to go back to re-strategise because they felt the new man would be a tough nut to crack.

The home based politicians were able to convince the "foreigner" that if he was ready to spend good money and grease necessary hands that victory would swing to his side, so everywhere Engineer gave $100 equivalent of their local currency, the "foreigner" dropped $500. The heat was too much on the engineer, the man was really upsetting his net and giving him the battle of his life, and the engineer had expended so much that it was too late for him to backout, the only alternative now was to pump more money into his campaign in order to maintain the lead. More money was needed to do another round of "oiling" which made him to sell all his houses in the country and the remaining two he had abroad, with the exception of the family mansion, he was now set to pursue the election vigorously. At last, victory was surely his, he won the election; but not a landslide victory as earlier envisaged.

The swearing-in was with pomp and glamour, his wife, kids, family, friends and political associates were all around to celebrate with him and the get-together after the official swearing-in was spectacular. Engineer though won the election, but he got to the government house partially broke! In fact, during the electioneering campaign, he sought the financial assistance of some female party members with the promise of paying back when he gets to office and also promised them political appointments.

On settling down in office, the first thing he did was to relocate his nine children abroad to continue with their studies so as to shield them from distraction; any way he could have still done this if he was not a provincial governor because he could afford it even then.

He picked all his aides and reneged on the promises he made to the two female politicians that helped him with finances, but he paid back their money with interests and made an arrangement with them to be fronting for him. The women didn't know each other's connection with the engineer, all they knew was that they were both party faithfuls and activists that contributed to the success of the election.

He was running the province to the best of his ability, with capable hands around him and giving all the plum contracts to the two female politicians as he had promised. They share the profits and keep Engineer's portion in the bank in trust for him and sometimes he would instruct them to use his share to buy properties on his behalf, but he doesn't want the properties and the bank accounts to be traceable to him. This they did, the titles to the properties were in different fictitious names and some in those women's names. Within three years of being the provincial controller, he was able to acquire thrice as much of what he used to have through the arrangements with the female politicians. Along the line, he began dating one of the women and promised her marriage after his tenure, this relationship was discovered by the second woman and she confronted the engineer, asking him if she was not beautiful enough that he had to go for the other woman. Initially, the engineer wanted to deny the allegation, but he had a rethink and apologised to her and declared "madam haba, don't you know that too much of women are not good and can destroy destiny", they both had a hearty laughter after which the engineer gave her a peck and she departed.

The woman started spying on the new lover and discovered that she too was fronting for the engineer as well, so she was not in the act alone. Amina was taking a good care of the home front shuttling between New York where their children were schooling and her country [home]. The engineer's mistress at the other end was pressurising him for marriage.

A year into the engineer's end of tenure, his lover informed him that she was pregnant, but this didn't go down well with the engineer who instructed her to terminate the pregnancy and pleaded with her to see reason because this might affect his fortune during his second term bid, as people might see him as an irresponsible fellow, he promised his mistress heaven and earth if she could accede to his demand. The engineer promised his mistress a huge sum of money, huge enough to acquire three magnificent mansions in his province. She was paid the huge sum and she travelled abroad only to come back after three weeks and informed her lover that she had done the abortion.

The "foreigner" that has been a pain on the neck of the engineer during his first electioneering campaigns, after losing the election refused to go back to his base, he desperately waited for the end of the engineer's tenure to try his luck again. His continuous staying in the country brought nightmares to Engineer, he did everything within his power to banish the "foreigner" out of his province and country but could not succeed. When the "foreigner" realised that his life was in danger, he relocated to the country's capital, but he still have his faithfuls on ground at his province as he had eventually became a force to reckon with in his province. It was getting into another election period, every politician needed to put his or her house and acts in order; in order to gain more ground and enlarge the camp of his faithful, the engineer made advances to the other female politician [Binta by name] to cement a proper relationship which she gladly consented to, at least this has been her life's dream. Having been banished from his province by the engineer's threats to go and settle in their country's capital, the "foreigner" who was not familiar with the terrain of his country because he had left his country for decades, now started mixing with other politicians and powerful power brokers in his country and thus becoming popular at the national level. Oh, level has changed the "foreigner" ceased from being a local champion, he now commands more influence around his country.

All hell was let loose, the unexpected happened the "foreigner" decamped from his not too popular party to Engineer's party. Engineer's camp had to rush back to the drawing board to see how the governorship slot would not slip out of their hands, but the battle for the party ticket was quite tough, even as an incumbent, Engineer couldn't get the party ticket for the second term. With the observation of their environment and the people, Engineer's camp came to the conclusion that with enough financial muscles anyone can win an election in their province, the poverty level is still very high and everybody are after their mouths and what they can get from the politicians, they defected from their party to a rival party and clinched the party's governorship slot.

Banking on the massive investments and funds he had with his mistresses, he called them on the need to transfer all the funds into a designated account for the purpose of the forthcoming election, he also instructed them to sell some of the properties and lodge the money into the same account, as if it was a planned thing, both women took the account details, promised to effect the transfer as soon as possible and left. [The meetings were held separately].

After a delay of about six days, the engineer called the second mistress [Binta] to inquire the reason for the delay in carrying out his instruction, Binta feigned ignorance as to what Engineer was talking about. She told him bluntly never to phone her again on any such issue that she could not understand what the engineer was talking about. He was speechless and shocked, he could not call out for help, his world was crumbling, he was flabbergasted and was afraid; he didn't know the next step to take; he landed in the hospital the following morning.

On his discharge from the hospital, he was dead afraid to call his first mistress wondering why she didn't visit him in the hospital knowing that Amina his wife had travelled to New York to visit the children. Eventually, he was able to summon up courage and contacted his mistress, she listened to him, but took him down the memory lane, how he promised her an appointment in exchange for the campaign money she borrowed him and he reneged, how he promised her marriage and upon pestering him, he did not budge and crowning it all; he insisted on her terminating the pregnancy she informed him of, at this juncture, she now let the cat out of the bag that she was not pregnant at all, that she just tested him and he failed woefully.

She gave the engineer a stern warning to let the meeting they had be their first and last on that issue and instructed him to destroy the duplicate titles of all the properties she had helped him to acquire because they were not authentic and if he liked he could cry out. Engineer's life was disappearing like a vapour in the air, he prostrated, sweating profusely pleading with his mistress to have a rethink and have mercy on him. At this point in time, Engineer knew he had come to the end of the road politically because all the money he had banked on to use in pursuing his second term election bid were gone. He therefore begged his mistress since his tenure was nine months to its expiration to release some funds to him to keep body and soul together but she was adamant and even threatened to cry out that he was after her life for no just cause. The engineer lost gallantly and his health failed because there were no funds to pursue his second term election bid. Due to lack of funds, the kids were relocated back to the country and fixed in a public school but not in their province anymore. Amina his wife had to go in search of work in order to put food on the family's table and keep it running. Out of fear of what the engineer might do to them, (the mistresses) threatened to expose him if he dared sending assassins after them. For the fear of the unknown and state prosecution coupled with the fact that he could not get help from friends and associates, and to avoid unnecessary embarrassment, the engineer fled abroad to take up odd jobs, he worked as a security man in the evening and drives a cab during the day in order to keep the body and soul together and his health continued to fail.

The family mansion was sold to buy a smaller house and the leftover from the sales was put to better use for theirs was really a large family, for the engineer, his experience was a slice of life.

The ravishing beauty was the talk of the town, anytime she appears on the social scene heads are turning, but really this babe was not carrying anything spectacular. A geologist by profession Aye, now in her 50s, who when she was in the second year in the high school gullibly followed five of her classmates to a herbalist's place in her village in search of fortune for good grades in school. When it got to Aye's turn, she asked for what would make her great not only in school, but in life. After series of incantation were chanted, the herbalist poured a liquid on her head and declared over her that people will go down for her sake and gave her a lotion to rub on her forehead for seven days, but she didn't tell her the repercussion of her demand.

On graduation from a university in France, she relocated to Ghana to practice and fortune actually smiled on her, life was rosy for her from day one. She got married at the age of 25 through traditional rite to a 35- year-old bank manager, married man and a father of three; of course she couldn't have had a court marriage because his man was still very much married to his first wife. What attracted this man to Aye, no man can tell because his wife was beautiful than Aye and even more successful, she was also the daughter of a top government functionary in their country. The bank manager packed out of his matrimonial home and moved in with Aye. The couple were so much in love that they became five and six in the city, making appearances at every city social gathering and business meetings and dinners, but as Aye's profile was soaring up that of her husband the bank manager was nose diving. On the long run, he lost his job with the bank and his personal investment was gone; his attempt to go back to his legal wife was rebuffed by her; she will not take him back. The guy was fed up with life, but Aye still wanted him, she was ready to keep him as her husband as she was not complaining at all; but he was not comfortable at all because his means of livelihood was gone, he was not contributing anything to the family purse. Inferiority complex will not allow him to have a peace of mind, he couldn't continue to stay under Aye's roof, he swallowed up his shame and went back to live in his parents' house.

At 28, Aye met a diplomat at a business meeting; after two weeks dating when she found out the married man was living alone, she moved in with him, the diplomat's wife was still in their home country planning to join her husband in his country of assignment later. Two years into her relationship with the diplomat, Aye made so much connections that changed her fortune for the better, she was thanking her star for the day she met the man and both were enjoying their relationship. Without any known ailment, the diplomat died suddenly in his sleep.

Aye relocated back to France where she had her university education, she was terribly sad and lonely she needed to be in the midst of her old friends and mates. More so she had opened a firm in Paris during her days with the diplomat and the outfit was doing fine. Adjusting to her new environment as a business woman in France and not a student this time around, she came in contact with one of her old classmates during their university days who was married to one of the top men in the country who invited her for dinner in her home and before the woman knew what was happening Aye has gotten pregnant for her husband. To save his marriage and his status in the society, he relocated Aye to the USA to cool off and have her baby. On delivery, she gave birth to a bouncing baby girl and shortly before the girl's first birthday, the man lost his prestigious job and life became unbearable for him and his family. He could not meet his financial obligations anymore Aye was now the one sending money to the father of her daughter to keep the body and soul together, without the knowledge of her friend, the man's wife.

At age 45, Aye got entangled with a top entertainer in the USA who showered her with so much love and affection at the expense of his wife of 15 years. Five months into their relationship, the man got involved in a car crash and died on the spot.

When Aye lost another wealthy lover of hers in a plane crash, she decided to take a stock of her life, it has now dawned on her that something was really wrong somewhere she declared to herself "why did I always end up in the hands of married men? Why do they always get into crisis once I'm in their lives and things always look up for me whatever the situation, three men had died in my hands, what might be responsible for these?". She later remembered what happened during her high school days in the village how she stupidly followed her mates to the herbalist place and all that took place, what kept coming back to her memory was what the herbalist pronounced on her "people will go down for your sake".

Where could she get help, she didn't know, to go back to the herbalist, she couldn't trace her way, she has lost all the contacts of the school mates she went with, to stay clear of men she cannot do.

That was how men that couldn't rule their systems died or crashed cheaply in the hands of Aye. As long as Aye couldn't find solution to her problems, more successful men will still fall in her hands.

12

"RECAPITALIZATION"

CHAPTER 12

===========================

"RECAPITALIZATION"

N o one needs to counsel the management of any organization that it's balance sheet is in deficit on what to do, if the Chief executive officer or the management team are experienced and not caricatures, with a glaring reality staring them in the face, the facts behind the figures are very clear, they either act fast in salvaging the situation or face bankruptcy.

It is always between the options of re- capitalization and insolvency, of course nobody wants to be thrown out of business unceremoniously they will choose the option of a great escape re- capitalization would offer them and get back to their beats, the same way with every individual who had been entangled in the wide web of "homogenous commodities" there is always a way of great escape, no reasonable person wants to go down in life when there is an option of staying afloat and getting ahead.

Life has thrown a beautiful option to every one of us and that is change.

Change simply means a movement from one state to another, something or someone or a situation or experience becoming different.

"The only two things that are permanent in life are TRUTH AND CHANGE".

You are the architect of your destiny, for you to attain and retain a lofty height in life and career, you have to embrace the truth and effect a change. Are we not lucky that at every junction in life we are permitted to make a U-turn or reconsider our stand? We have a free choice to make at every point in time if we feel like. Life is about making choices, so we have a great personal contribution to how we turnout in life, we have the power from within and without on how we want our end product to be. Every human being have a level of control over their system, "I cannot control myself outburst is not tenable". Seeing a lovely naked lady by the road side beckoning on you, would you have come down from your car and remove your pants to go into her right there? Of course not, "that can never happen" is the answer you will give. That means you have self-control, you can walk away in the face of any pressure. The fact that you won't grab a babe in public glare to have sex with her no matter how much you are in "love" [lust], you are able to hold yourself for a conducive time and place to carry out your agenda shows that you have control over your system, so, relatively you can rule your body and your world to a large extent.

Still on the issue of ruling your system, no man will fall for any babe that he knows of her positive Human Immunodeficiency Virus(HIV) status even if he is in a serious lust you will hold yourself to look for an alternative.

Recognising you have a problem with "homogeneous commodities" and taking responsibility is your first step to recovery. If you argue that the 'altar' is not your problem that it is the packaging then all you need do is having many of them around you at every point in time and be relishing yourself in their beauty and charms and not temper with the product.. Once you recognise that the "homogeneous commodity" [the product] that the possessor carries is your problem then solution is knocking at your door. I'm restating here that what is crumbling your world is a commodity that is the same thing the world over, it is homogeneous once you have one, you don't need a second one otherwise people will see you as a mad fellow. That 'item' is a mystery and sacred, be satisfied with the one you have, acquiring one is acquiring all.

Acknowledge the need to be free, if you don't take the bull by the horns then forget having the bull to yourself. The need to be free has to be pursued vigorously because some people are free, so why not you? Some are not entangled at all, why should you? These are the questions you should be asking yourself. Don't be deceived that every other person is in your shoes or every other people have been in your shoes. Deception is the mother of destruction.

Another question that is worth asking yourself is, why will I labour from childhood to adulthood to achieve success, fame, and honour only to use my own hand to scatter them at the altar of an "item" that is legally available to me, an "item" that I have, that is just the same thing as my neighbour's and is not even scarce if I need to get one legitimately?

Only a nincompoop will ignore the need to be free and I'm sure you are not one. You have paid your dues in life and you should know that freedom is sweet and awesome.

Having recognised the problem and acknowledged the need to be free, there is the need to go to your manufacturer with your facts at hand before you present and defend your case.

Manufacturers are the creative architects of a product. They know why they put this nut before that nut; they know all the nitty-gritty of the products they sent to the market place because this world is a market place where any kind of buying and selling are taking place. There have been occasions where manufacturers recall some products they have sold out, most times because of errors detected during usage. Why do you think they didn't instruct the users to send them to any repairer or garages near them? Because they know those repairers cannot do a thorough job, they don't have the original formula or master plan as to correct those errors. They assembled those products in the first place and they are the ones that can adjust and fix them perfectly.

Your manufacturer knows you more than anyone else because he was the one that fix every item in your body in the first place and if you observed any defect, common sense demands he should be your first port of call. Never make a mistake of calling on anyone before you sort out your case with your maker, he has your master plan and he alone knows what is needed to be fixed or serviced in your system that will cause it to work honourably, He ALONE has the prerogative of mercy.

He alone can unscramble your heavens that has been scrambled up through illegal involvement with "homogeneous commodities" your maker has your system anatomy he made you, so seeking help from other sources before consulting him is like embarking on a suicide mission, please don't. He knows all the components of your system and he is in a better position to reset and do the necessary adjustments. Don't allow anybody to lure you into seeking help from a mortal being before getting instruction from your manufacturer. How do you even know that the so called helper is not battling with the same issue you are facing? Your manufacturer is in a better position to direct you on how to tackle the situation. The way out of your issue is better sorted out between the two of you or he might instruct you to where to get help, if seeking external help will solve the problem.

When you buy a Mercedes Benz product you take it to the company's designated garage for complaints and repairs, the same thing with Kia, Ford, Bmw, and Rolls Royce. It will be out of place to take a Bmw product to Kia garage for fixing, if you do that, they cannot give you a satisfactory service and you cannot be satisfied, though they might have an idea because they are equally engineers, but that is not their area of specialisation. Your car will still give you problems after a while. So, do the right things at every point in time, put a round peg into a round hole and the solution will be a permanent and lasting one. There is always a huge danger in seeking external help without first getting the nod of your maker as to the path to tread in freeing yourself.

Identifying how you actually landed yourself in your present predicament will be an added advantage in your pursuit of freedom. In identifying this you can guide against its reoccurrence and take precautions. You might need to drop some friends, you might need to reduce your presence from certain circles, and it might even be more boldness and brushing up your self-esteem that is needed.

Forgiving yourself is a crucial step in getting your freedom. Guilt can really weighs one down and to think soundly becomes a problem. When you forgive yourself, the first thing you will notice is that you won't dwell much on your shortcomings, you will be able to laugh at your mistakes and misfortunes. Boldness comes for you to gain back your momentum and set out again to make progress in life. Never allow a pity party around you! We are all work in progress, so don't be overwhelmed by your shortcomings. If tortoise didn't pick up the pieces of his hunch back, it could have faced extinction by now, but he did that and got himself back on his feet, though all the cracks are still visible till today, at least the scars will remind him of how not to cheat on others.

Another major step to "recapitalization" especially for those in a legal union is to confide in their spouses before things get out of hands and seek for their spouses forgiveness and cooperation if need be. In dealing properly with this I think the anatomy of human brains [both male and female] and how they work need to be discussed briefly because it is expedient for each party to have an understanding in this field as to adjust to the reality on ground, for in knowing this, each party will know the level of compromise and understanding to give into the "recapitalization" process.

Woman's Brain

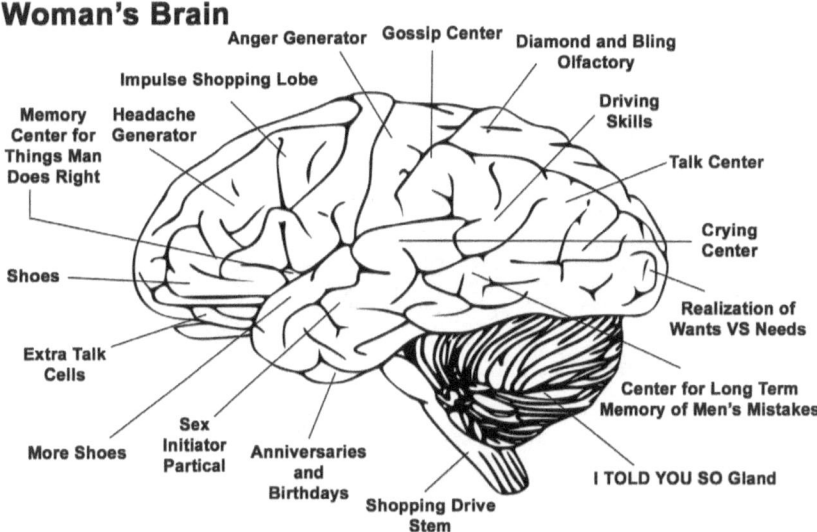

NOTE: The "Put Gas in the Car" and the "Be Quiet during the Game or Movie" glands are only active when the Diamond and Bling Olfactory has been satisfied or when there is a shoe sale!

Women's brain is created by the manufacturer in such a way that everything is connected to each other at the same time. Everything in a woman's brain is connected to everything, that is, interwoven so all their senses are working together at the same time. That is why a woman can do a lot of things at the same time, their brains are ever working, their brains never shutdown. Technically this implies that with the formation of their brains no one thing can preoccupy them at the same time, with this uniqueness they are able to balance many issues at the same time. The working of everyone's brain determines the manifestations of their actions.

DIFFERENCES BETWEEN THE MAN AND WOMAN BRAINS

Man's Brain

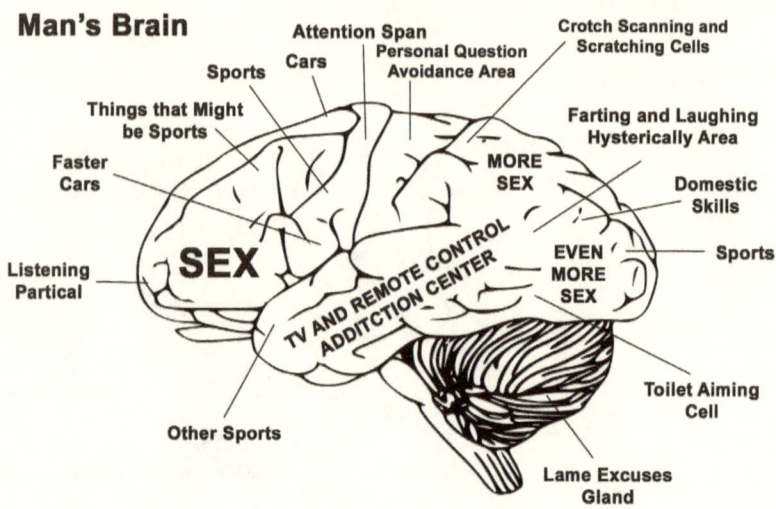

Attention Span
Personal Question Avoidance Area
Crotch Scanning and Scratching Cells
Sports
Cars
Things that Might be Sports
Farting and Laughing Hysterically Area
Faster Cars
MORE SEX
Domestic Skills
Listening Partical
SEX
TV AND REMOTE CONTROL ADDITCTION CENTER
EVEN MORE SEX
Sports
Other Sports
Toilet Aiming Cell
Lame Excuses Gland

Woman's Brain

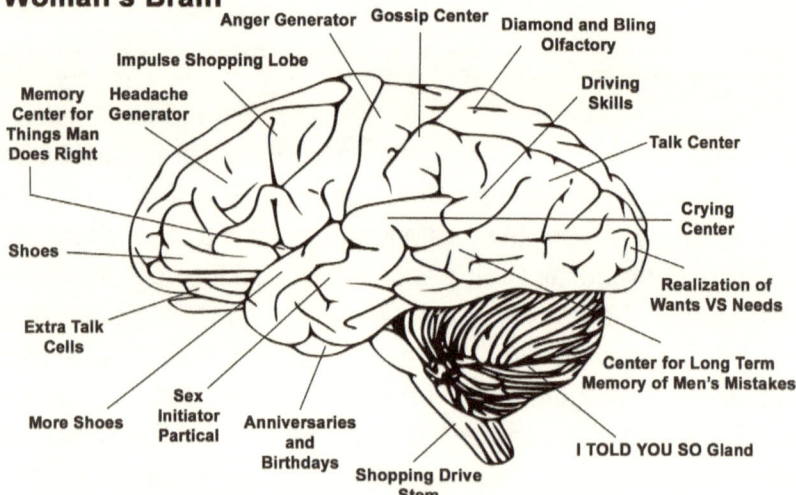

Anger Generator
Gossip Center
Diamond and Bling Olfactory
Impulse Shopping Lobe
Driving Skills
Memory Center for Things Man Does Right
Headache Generator
Talk Center
Shoes
Crying Center
Extra Talk Cells
Realization of Wants VS Needs
More Shoes
Sex Initiator Partical
Anniversaries and Birthdays
Center for Long Term Memory of Men's Mistakes
Shopping Drive Stem
I TOLD YOU SO Gland

NOTE: The "Put Gas In the Car" and the "Be Quiet during the Game or Movie" glands are only active when the Diamond and Bling Olfactory has been satisfied or when there is a shoe sale!

For a man's brain the functioning is entirely different and in fact it is the opposite, we must be careful here to note that the manufacturer didn't make any mistake here, that is how he wanted it to be and we have to accept it as such.

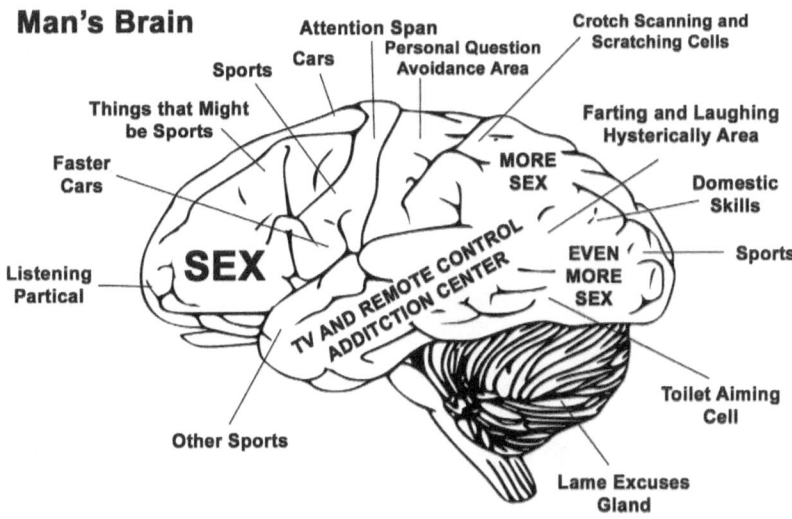

Man's Brain

Attention Span
Personal Question Avoidance Area
Cars
Sports
Crotch Scanning and Scratching Cells
Things that Might be Sports
Farting and Laughing Hysterically Area
Faster Cars
MORE SEX
Domestic Skills
Listening Partical
SEX
TV AND REMOTE CONTROL ADDITCTION CENTER
EVEN MORE SEX
Sports
Toilet Aiming Cell
Other Sports
Lame Excuses Gland

A man's brain cannot do a lot of things at the same time, it is one thing per time, that implies if it is engrossed in a certain task he needs to shutdown that department of his brain first before he can shift to another department say home affairs or family life. As I have discussed earlier under women's brain that the workings of everyone's brain determines their manifestations and their actions, a spouse that does not understand or has knowledge of the working of his or her partner's brain is bound to pick quarrels at every point because he or she would feel the partner was not doing enough in handling situations and issues, it is always comments like ; "you should have it at the back of your mind when making that purchase that, that is not what we need now", "you should have it at the back of your mind while working in the office that the gas cylinder is still at the gas station". All these "you should have" lists are endless in homes and these are indirectly having a negative effects on your relationships and sex lives if you believe it or not, before you know it resentments has crept into the union.

From the above diagrams' illustrations you can see the compartments and the size the manufacturer gave to each item in a man's brain. Work life have it's own compartment, family and home life has their own compartments, sex life has it's own compartment and the vacuum [empty] section has it's own compartment too. It will be shocking that the largest functioning compartment in a man's brain is the section housing their sex life, the other large compartment is the empty portion, that is why atimes when you ask a man about what his thought is at a certain moment, he might tell you he's not thinking about anything and this seldom create a sort of distrust between spouses because a woman that is not knowledgeable on the working of a man's brain might think her spouse is hiding something from her, she will find it very difficult to fathom that a person can sit down or awake and not thinking about anything because she feels every brain is working like her own but the truth of the matter is that he's not thinking about anything, when his senses are in the empty compartment, he's blank and true to his word he is not thinking about anything.

The other large compartment which houses the sex life of a man accounts for the largest functioning compartment in a man's brain anatomy. If the compartment that houses a man's sex life is then the largest functioning compartment of a his brain then men's often demand for sex should not be considered as a weakness on their part, the real weakness is in the inability to control their libido, that is the way they were wired, we need to mind our comments, accept and respect them and their manufacturer, most notably, the man's brain is generally and directly connected to a penis by involved systems.

This is the juncture where spouses compromise and understanding comes to bear, both parties should be able to work out a relationship template where an equilibrium sex level can be attained, that is the demand for sex in a legal union must be equal to the supply. An economy is said to be at equilibrium at the point where allocation of goods is at its most efficient because the amount of goods being supplied is exactly the same as the amount being demanded, thus every party is satisfied. In a nutshell this scenario is a favourable economic state and this can be applied in a legal union as well, the demand for sex within a union must be equal to the supply within the same union if "recapitalization" process must be successful, disequilibrium sexual state should not be encourage within a union.

As long as a disequilibrium sexual state is prevalent in a home, recapitalization process becomes a herculean task, it would be like keeping a pet in the house and you are not feeding it as at when due or you are starving it of food, before you know what is happening the pet will be escaping from where it is kept, wandering around for food and when it is satisfied outside it would trace his way back to the house at night to sleep, and this routine becomes it lifestyle.

(turnover leaf to have a look at what an equilibrium graph looks like in order to have clearer understanding)

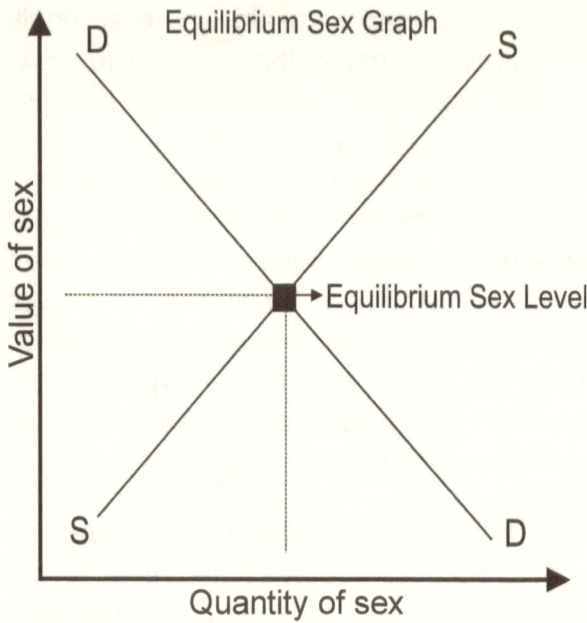

Relationship template is not something you just discuss casually over dinner it is something that you need to make a conscious and consented effort to address, it is a serious 'boardroom' meeting that requires a roundtable discussion and tackling between the two major stakeholders. Each party should table how they wanted to be treated within their union and since both parties now have a proper understanding of how each partner's brain functions and why it is functioning that way, the often complains on women's part of men's insatiable demands for sex can be tackled and handled wisely and either party will not feel guilty of any kind of insensitivity to each other.

The five major love languages must come to bear at this "board meeting"

1 WORD OF AFFIRMATION
2 QUALITY TIME
3 ACTS OF SERVICE
4 GIFTS
5 PHYSICAL TOUCH.

Each partner should be able to discuss which of these five options [love languages] will enhance their sexual desires for each other freely, an enabling environment must be created by both parties for utmost sexual satisfaction within the union. For some it may be through words of affirmation from their spouses that enhances their sexual desire, for some it may be an option of having a quality time together.

Acts of service from either of the partner could be the magic wand in some union, it might be physical touch or exchange of gifts for some other unions but the crucifix of the matter is that all avenues must be exploited to create a sex life equilibrium within a legal union in order to tackle this 'menace' that is pulverizing colorful destinies into powder and grinding great and brilliant careers into smithereens.

Do not hold back if there is a need to discuss the issue with friends and colleagues, there might be some that have overcame the issue you are battling and can be of help.

Work on your thought pattern, let the thoughts of righteousness flow into your heart any time you are attracted to a "processor", or better still tag the "processor" to your family members like your wife, mother, sister, daughter or cousin. "Oh, she's like my sister; oh her legs are like that of my mummy". Her carriage is just like my grandmother's; oh, her boobs are just like my wife's". With these thoughts on your mind, the temptation to trespass is drastically reduced.

Having stated the ways to recovery, the truth about every human misfortune and the reason why they find themselves in their present predicament is that they ignored the manufacturer's instructions manual when setting out in life; you think you are sensible enough and can figure out things on your own. The reason the manufacturer took his time to attach an instruction manual to his products in the first place is because he knows the buyer has sense and when reading the manual he or she can comprehend what was written there. He wouldn't have attached the instruction manual if he's selling to morons.

Go and check any product, I mean the genuine ones; the first thing you will see on it is "read the manufacturer instruction manual before use". There is no authentic product that doesn't have a manufacturer instruction manual attached to it. So if you have set out without reading or understanding your manufacturer's instruction manual, it is never too late you can go back to the drawing board and familiarise yourself with the manufacturer's manual.

Technologies, inventions, and discoveries to aid you in experiencing ultimate sexual pleasure with your legitimate partner abound, find out the ones that will suit you and your partner which are not offensive to your religious beliefs, seek the advice of experts in this field.

If after numerous deliveries [after birth effects], you feel that you are not experiencing the kind of pleasure you would have love to with your legitimate spouse due to the expansion of the vagina passage, there are herbal discoveries and knowledge on elasticity of vagina passages for expansion or contraction. The option of a Kegel exercise for vaginas tightening can also be explored.

EPILOGUE

I sat down in my gazebo gazing like a gazelle
beholding the evil that goes on under the sun.
A commodity that is homogeneous and readily available
if there is a need to acquire one legitimately
has been turned into an "altar" that is sniffing life
out of the poor, the rich, the nobles and the plebeians.

There I ponder on the wonders of creation,
a "commodity" that is common to all men
has been turned into an 'altar' that alters human
destinies met for good for evil.

An "altar" where the nobles chose to walk
into with a closed eyes as in walking into a gutter.
An "altar" where the low born loiter into
with a cloak on their eyes as in walking into a gutter.
An "altar" where nobles and the low born
that were not born blind from birth
falls into as in falling into a gutter.

Whoever falls into a gutter falls into
a surface below ground level,
no one goes into one without his garment being soiled.
This "altar" sinks whoever falls into it
like a gutter never without a stain and
some bruises when coming out.

Vagina Homogeneity

Injury may be fatal
Injury might be minor
but it must surely leave a scar.

Recovery may be slow
Recovery might be rapid
but definitely a wound has been established.

The "altar" is like a gutter always below
the ground surface in wrecking it's havoc
not on the ground surface where everyone can see.
As a gutter takes you below, the "altar" takes you beneath
causing you to grope in darkness like a groggy being.

I thought the nobles are the custodians of wisdom and nobility,
not until I see the nobles nobbled by the "altar",
the Nobs and the noble men are not exceptions.

The "altar" that levels the nobles and nobodies
a no respecter of the stray
a grinding machine that grinds greatness to granules.
At this "altar" every mountain becomes a mole
Every mole smashes in smithereens.
This "altar" rubbishes the rubies and disdains the dainty.
Discolorations of destinies are discovered at its doorsteps.
Degradation of destinies dangle on the necks of all its visitors.
The nobles throw caution to the wind at the "altar"
turning themselves into wobbling wolves.
The low born having no identity to lose on the field
takes caution for fear of juggle justice,
lurking around in a creepy manner for a proper time to strike.

The way to the "shrine" that housed the "altar"
is wide but I noticed the way the noble,
the royal, the plebeian and the low born
walk into it are the same, they all SNEAK.

Sneaking, slinking, tiptoeing and bend walking
are the habits of all the visitors,
never have I noticed any of those walking tall
on their shoulders on their ways to the "shrine".

The "shrine" is the house
the "altar" is the "commodity"
and the "'possessor" is the occupant.
Sneaking, slinking in a Sneaker that will not
make their movement heard,
normal shoes can give them away.

The sound of the noble's shoes herald their arrival,
the real leather sole will refuse to keep quiet
because all and sundry must notice it's super craftsmanship.
Towns and villages will know a noble has entered
the community but Sneakers are rubber soled touching sands
and grounds without making the slightest sound.

The low born too has caught the Sneakers bug,
sneaking in Sneakers because the nails the cobbler used
in mending his shoes will make noise that will give him away.
Sneaking and slinking in a pair of Sneakers
in a sneaky move devoid of any noise or sound.

The thought of the nobles being noble than
the low born collapsed on my face when I see the evil
going on under the sun over "homogeneous commodities".

They both with their eyes wide opened
match down to the "junction" where destinies
are pulverized with ease and
life long careers crushed effortlessly.

Vagina Homogeneity

Strange! Strange! Strange! Strange! Strange!
The nobles and low born make necessary effort
to create an enabling environment for the
crushing of their colorful destinies
without any help from family and friends
because it is a sneaking adventure,
no one is permitted to know.

"I must sneak to the "shrine" alone because the "altar"
is specially reserved for me".
Declared the nobles and the low born,
oblivious of the fact that as they are
sneaking in and sneaking out,
others too are sneaking out and sneaking in
out of the same "shrine".
Multiples are matching in and out to have
their destinies thoroughly pulverized.

The "junction" is a junction of grand deception and delusion
that grinds the giants to grains and the mole into millet.
It's a sneaking game everyone is sneaking and slinking.
No one is observant, for observation carries patience with it,
it has to cost you some time to watch for any danger ahead in
this sneaky moves.

Observation cannot be cost effective
it might cost you the unexpected
all movements must happen at the speed of a light.

This "junction" is the junction of head on collision
with destruction and disgrace !
Under this sun again I see the royals
throwing off their royal regalias
to taste out of the "altar" in the "shrine".

Royal regalia and all the grace and honor it
carries with it has no place and no meaning to them
where the "altar" is concerned.

The royals shed himself of his grace and honor
for a temporary sack cloth to avoid being noticed
when on a mission to the "shrine" that housed the "altar"
damning the security implication of his actions.

Grace, honour and security are the least on his agenda
when embarking on this suicide mission
when the unexpected happens
it's surely a spell from the detractors.

At the "altar" dignity and honour can go to blazes
because the senses had gone on recess,
the royal and the noble chose to embrace disgrace and dishonor
for a momentary gratification, groping in darkness
confusing retrogression with progression.

The low born too sheds himself of his sack cloth,
putting on a fine linen to present himself appealing
to the "possessor" of the "altar" as to confuse the
neighborhood inhabitants that a decent and honourable
man has come calling.

For the royal, the noble, and the low born it is always
the game of shedding, shedding, shedding.

Licking from the "altar" pot is sweet to the nobles
and the plebeians, they cannot lick their five fingers
enough without the oil on their singlet giving them away.
For the nobles it is always the excuse of numerous nocturnal
meetings that will move the province forward.
For the plebeians the strange movements is to make
sure they put an end to the vicious circle of poverty

that has engulfed their households.
An excuse must be given but it has to be one that is
far from the truth.

Death is a common denominator between the nobles
and the plebeians but I have also discovered another
common denominator among them, it is the suspension
of brain when at the "altar", senses and reasoning must
definitely go on vacation at that point in time.
It is always the sabbatical period for rational conducts.

The nobles and the plebeians always think because
they are on top they are in charge, forgetting the nature
facts that whoever is alert is the one in charge and on top.
The one at alert owns the game and call the shots,
destinies and careers are made or maimed at her caprice and
whim.

Another strange thing I observe under the sun is
the nobles and the plebeians that are not on special duties
or rendering emergency services turning themselves into
nocturnal beings navigating every nooks and crannies
without being a bat.

Another strange thing are the nobles and the plebeians
toiling from cradle to childhood then to adulthood
having achieved greatness, honor, dignity, riches, and
success only to turn their backs to such lofty heights
and embrace the "altar" whose sole assignment is to
grind destinies to a halt and sinks one to the swamp of despair.
This is strange and evil
whoever is led astray by the "altar"
is not wise.

I have seen a lifetime of toiling and
hard work collapsing like a pack
of cards at the "altar".

I have seen nobles with credible credentials through
commission or omission mortgaged them at the 'altar'.
As a flourescent attracts a moth
and leads it to an unexpected and horrifying end
so also the "altar" attracts those who seek
it with equally tragic results.

I have seen a royal riding on his royal horse with all
his entourage only for him to descend from his royal horse
to visit the "shrine" that housed the "altar"
and couldn't ascend back on his royal horse
his decision to descend leads to descent to oblivion.
I have also seen a royal that decided to descend and
upon ascending couldn't get back his throne.

I have seen a majesty that decided to descend and
in the process lost his crown.
I have also seen a warlord with all his paraphernalia
of office combined with his military might and exploits who
chose to descend but couldn't come out alive.

I have seen foremost statesmen that descended
and became laughing stocks before all and sundry.
I have also seen nationalists that took
the option of descending and their dignities riddled with ridicule.

I have seen political rivals employing the weapon of the 'altar'
to take dominion from their opponents.
A 'night encounter' with a planted possessor took away
the election result victory,
electorates waiting eagerly for the D- day to troop
out to elect their candidate of preference without

knowing that the election victory results has been
declared at the 'night of encounter'
when the dominion was wickedly taken away at the 'altar'.

I also heard it in history that Samson too lost it all at the 'altar'.

I have seen a head of government that chose to descend
and to ascend became a herculean task for him because
he got caught in the process.
I have also seen a head of corporation who descends
and bade goodbye to a promising career.

I have seen a king that chose to descend and escorted
back into his kingdom naked.
I have also seen a king that descended and ran out
of the "shrine" mad and naked.

I have seen a royalty that picked the option of descending
and somersaulted seven times nakedly to his grave.
Whoever is led astray by the "altar" is not wise.

The low born need not descend because they are already
on the ground level but I have seen a low born that
embraces the "altar" and embraced death.
I have seen a low born that embraces the "altar"
and embraced sickness.

I have seen a plebeian that embraces the "altar"
and embraced unimaginable wealth for a period of
eight months and at every eight months intervals he buried
his eight sons and a whole lineage was wiped out.
I have also seen a plebeian even in his lowest level
maintaining a three square meal daily routine and upon
embracing the "altar" a cup of water became a luxury
at his table.

I have heard of a low born thinking he was wise and
smartly tapped into the opportunity of a "commodity"
and turned into a money spinning commodity itself.
I have seen a low born embracing the "commodity" alone
and his whole household carried into captivity forever.

Embracing the "altar" is embracing self imposed captivity
Embracing the "altar" is embracing lifetime captivity
Whoever is led astray by the "altar" is not wise.

My utmost desire is
for all men to be free
V.H
available

@...

www.ingramcontent.com/pod-product-compliance
Lightning Source LLC
Chambersburg PA
CBHW050406290526
45786CB00003B/1147